HEATHROW CHICAGO

STANLEY STEWART

First published 1984

ISBN 0 7110 1434 5

© Ian Allan Ltd 1984

18502604

Published by Ian Allan Ltd, Shepperton, Surrey; and printed by Ian Allan Printing Ltd at their works at Coombelands in Runnymede, England.

Acknowledgements

A publication of this nature is normally a team effort and this book is no exception. A special word of thanks must go to the photographer, Peter Pugh, for producing such a wonderful set of prints. I would also like to thank all those below. The names are given 'in order of appearance', which, very conveniently, places the ladies first.

London
My sister Dorothy Wallace for her tireless effort in typing the manuscript; Andrea Thomas for her enthusiastic guidance in improving my English; Senior First Officer Mike Chan-Choong; Senior Engineer Officers Peter Carrigan and Simon Robinson, and Ground Engineer Henry (John) Metcalfe for their advice on technical matters; and Mr Ted Duggan, British Airways Press Office, for his help in arranging the flight for the photographer. All those on the crew to Chicago, especially Captain Edward Murray for his kindness and help with the photography on the flight deck and advice on the manuscript; Senior Engineer Officer Phil Roberts, also for his help with the photography and advice on the manuscript; Cabin Services Officer Eddie Crockford for his guidance on cabin procedures; and Stewardess Sue Latham for her help with the photography during the meal service. Captain Peter Royce, British Airway's 747 Fleet Manager, and, of course, British Airways for permission to publish.

Chicago
All the British Airways' staff at O'Hare, especially Station Duty Officer Eric Patterson for arranging the control tower visit; Ground Engineer Carl Rawls for his kindness and help with the photography at the airport; and last but not least, the controllers in the tower at O'Hare for their friendliness and help with the photography.

Abbreviations

ADF	automatic direction finder
ASI	airspeed indicator
ATC	air traffic control
ATIS	automatic terminal information service
°C	degrees centigrade
CAA	Civil Aviation Authority
CAT	clear air tubulence
CSO	Cabin Services Officer
DME	distance measuring equipment
EGT	exhaust gas temperature
EPR	engine pressure ratio
°F	degrees Fahrenheit
FAA	Federal Aviation Authority
GMT	Greenwich mean time
HF	high frequency
HP	high pressure
ICAO	International Civil Aviation Authority
ILS	instrument landing system
INS	inertial navigation system
KHz	kilohertz
Met	meteorology
MHz	megahertz
N_1	engine fan
N_2	engine high pressure compressor
Nav	navigation
NDB	non-directional beacon
nm	nautical miles
PA	public address system
PNdB	perceived noise decibels
RMI	radio magnetic indicator
R/T	radio telephony
SID	standard instrument departure
V_1, V_2	take-off speeds
V_R	rotation (lift-off) speed
VHF	very high frequency
VOR	very high frequency omni-directional radio range

HEATHROW...

If a darts player were to aim at a map of North America and strike the bull dead centre, the dart would land remarkably close to Chicago. In fact, to be absolutely accurate, the city of Chicago does lie somewhat due east of the mid-point of the Northern Continent, but its position as centre of the industrial and agricultural heartland of America is undisputed. From its earliest days Chicago has been a major transport centre, first of road and rail, and now as the hub of a giant aviation network with spokes touching every corner of the Americas and the far flung globe beyond. Not surprisingly the airport of Chicago, O'Hare, with its vast national and international traffic, is the busiest commercial jet centre in the world. On average an aircraft arrives or departs from its runways every 50 seconds.

On the opposite side of the Atlantic, at the busiest *international* airport in the world, on a cold damp Saturday afternoon in February, a British Airways Boeing 747, Flight Number 298, prepares to depart from London, Heathrow, for the snow-threatened expanse of Chicago, O'Hare. By day's end yet another movement will have been added to the already impressive traffic figures of both airports. O'Hare boasts a staggering total of almost 605,000 movements per year with Heathrow well down the list at around 270,000 public transport movements. London's international status, however, is indicated by the number of large longhaul jet transport movements, a tenth of the world's jumbo fleet being found there on any one day. Passenger figures reflect Heathrow's status as third busiest in terms of people handled with just over 26.4million per year compared to O'Hare's 37.9million. Atlanta, Hartsfield, in Georgia lies a close second with 37.6million.

Scheduled departure time for BA298 is 1415 GMT with arrival in Chicago at 1645 local time. On the mainland United States, longitudinal separation between east and

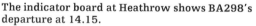

destination	time	flight number	information	
OSLO	13:50	BA 644	LAST CALL	GATE
AMSTERDAM	14:15	BA 414		
CHICAGO	14:15	BA 298	NOW BOARDING GATE	
STOCKHOLM	14:25	BA 652		
PARIS	14:30	BA 312		
MILAN	14:35	BA 512		
VIENNA	14:45	BA 604		
ROME	14:55	BA 504		
GENEVA	15:00	BA 626		
COPENHAGEN	15:10	BA 638		
HAMBURG	15:15	BA 736		
GOTHENBURG	15:20	BA 658		

Above:
The indicator board at Heathrow shows BA298's departure at 14.15.

west coasts is large enough to require four time zones to encompass the continent — Eastern, Central, Mountain and Pacific at −5, −6, −7 and −8 respectively from GMT in winter. Chicago lies in the Central time zone at −6, so BA 298's arrival at O'Hare will be at 2245 GMT. (In summer daylight saving applies and times from GMT are one hour less.)

At present London time is 1315 with one hour remaining to departure. Most passengers are required to check in a minimum of 60 minutes before the flight and many of 298's travellers are already proceeding through the departure lounge. At check-in individual pieces of luggage are weighed and average weights for each passenger and hand baggage — males 78kg, females 68kg, children 43kg and infants 10kg — are passed, together with seat allocation, to the computer for analysis. Fuel figures and cargo loading details are also fed by the respective departments to the computer and all information on loads, distribution and aircraft trim are later presented

Above:
Passenger check-in at Terminal 1 — males 78kg, females 68kg . . .

Right:
Passengers view 'november juliet' from the departure lounge.

for inspection to the Captain, in the form of a load sheet, just before departure.

In operations the staff have already prepared details of the flight and today's Captain, Edward Murray, and his crew of Co-pilot, Senior First Officer Stan Stewart, and Flight Engineer, Senior Engineer Officer Phil Roberts, are examining the information presented before acceptance. Previously each had made his way independently to the crew car park in the British Airways maintenance area on the east side of the airport. From there the three were transported by company car to the central area to report for duty in Queens Building one hour before departure. Now, at the 'Atlantic' desk in operations, the paperwork is spread before them.

On flights to the States in winter, weather is of prime importance, and destination and diversion airport forecasts are viewed with interest. At arrival time in Chicago the figures indicate a cloud cover of ⅝th stratocumulus at 2,000ft with the possibility of snow showers.

Snow is common in North America in winter and severe snow storms can close major airports over half the Eastern Continent within a matter of hours. Snow, in fact, is Chicago airport's biggest problem, and O'Hare has been known to be shut for up to three days as a result of a heavy fall.

Weather in the mid-US is typically continental with extremes of climate, and, strange as it may seem, weather conditions there, as in many other parts of the world, are often dictated more by geographical environment than by latitude. Consider, for a moment, the heating effect of the sun. Air is a poor conductor of heat (ie it absorbs heat slowly) so the warmth we feel on the ground is heat which is first absorbed by the earth's surface before being radiated, or thrown out, into the atmosphere. In summer, when the sun is more directly overhead, a large land mass affords good surface heating and high radiation results in hot sticky summers. With the sun low in the sky in winter, surface heating is reduced, and bitterly cold winters result. Latitude, of course, does play a part, the more northerly cities being generally colder than those further south, but comparisons between positions at the same latitude in different parts of the hemisphere can throw up some surprises. New York, for example, is on the same latitude as Madrid. Snow and bitterly cold temperatures are not uncommon in New York, but there would be more than a few shocked Spaniards if a foot of snow suddenly fell in the bullring!

Wind forecasts for arrival time in O'Hare indicate strong southeasterlies (ie wind blowing from the SE) backing to northeast, gusting from 15 to 20kt, and come as no surprise. Chicago, lying exposed at the edge of the prairie lands on the south western tip of Lake Michigan, is well known as the 'windy city', and like many other North American cities conditions are affected as a result. In summer the tall buildings form a barrier against the light winds and inner areas are hot, humid and polluted. In winter the strong winds funnel between the tower blocks with a force which can knock a man down, the effective temperatures plummeting 20 or 30°F with the added influence of the wind chill factor. In Boston the windows of one futuristic glass skyscraper were sucked from their frames when the wind blew from a particular direction at above a certain strength. On such days whole streets were cordoned off to protect the public. As each giant pane smashed to the ground it was replaced by a large wooden panel until there was so much wood in the building the fire department declared it a fire hazard!

The fuel flight plan is also examined and is seen to designate Detroit as diversion airport, but with possible snow falls over most of the area the eastern seaboard cities are also inspected. Boston is out, with forecast cloud cover of $^8/_8$ths (ie total cloud cover) nimbostratus at 500ft and visibility of one mile in snow, which is below the diversion airport weather minima (ie minimum limits) of 800ft cloud base and visibility two statute miles. New York is better, with $^5/_8$ths stratocumulus at 3,500ft, fresh westerly winds, and rain showers. Even with minimum fuel an en route diversion to New York is possible. Detroit lies 245 miles due east of Chicago with

Fig 1:
Fuel flight plan.

similar weather, but the forecast for both airports indicates only a 40% probability of light snow showers, so should not pose a problem. Montreal and Toronto are also both passed en route and are showing favourable weather. All flights must carry diversion fuel, even if destination weather is forecast to be fine, and weather and commercial desirability both play a part in the selection of an alternative. Nominating Havana, for example, as diversion airport from Miami would have more than a few passengers nervous if the weather were bad over Florida and the aircraft actually did divert to Cuba. That would be one way of ensuring that a plane load of people never flew with your airline again! Detroit, of course, lies fairly close to Chicago, and could cause problems if severe weather affected both airports. Today's weather prospects are reasonable, but Detroit is still a doubtful alternative to the Captain in these forecast conditions. It is noted from the fuel flight plan that an extra 2.4tonnes carried brings Minneapolis/St Pauls within range as a diversion and in the interests of safety this is added to the fuel figure. It is also considered that landing delays may be a problem with snow forecast, and a decision is made to carry full contingency fuel as a precaution. Since only enough fuel is carried for flight requirements it's imperative that sufficient is on board. North Atlantic route fuel requirements are normally around the 100tonne figure, but the maximum fuel capacity of the Pratt and Whitney-engined Boeing 747 is nearer 140 tonnes, which is equivalent to the total weight of a fully laden and fuelled Boeing 707.

A final check is made of the computed fuel flight plan figures, and the calculations scanned for error. The total fuel figure required of 106 tonnes comprises 86.1 tonnes for the flight, 14.6 tonnes diversion fuel for Minneapolis/St Pauls or Detroit, Metro Wayne County (just in case), 4.3 tonnes contingency fuel to allow for flight level changes, adverse winds, landing delays, etc, and one tonne of fuel for taxi at London.

Upper air charts are also inspected for upper winds, forecast clear air tubulence, and any significant weather expected en route, while an examination of the flight notices shows nothing of note which may prevent departure — such as airspace restrictions or airports closed, etc. At Chicago it is noted that runway 14 left/32 right is closed and some minor light systems and one radio frequency are unserviceable at New York. Heathrow, jokingly referred to as the only airport operating in the middle of a building site, has the usual information on work in progress at various points.

The flight logs for the complete journey must also be checked against the air traffic control flight plan routeing which is filed with air traffic control by operations staff before departure. The requested routeing is on airways White 22 and Upper Amber 2 to Deans Cross on the Scottish border, then Upper White 14 to Machrihanish on the Mull of Kintyre. At this point the Atlantic crossing commences on track co-ordinates 56 N 10 W, 57 N 20 W, 58 N 30 W, 58 N 40 W, 58 N 50 W, to Prawn, then to Schefferville in northern Labrador (Newfoundland), Canada, and by North American route 324 to Chicago. North Atlantic tracks are selected twice daily by computer to follow best winds, or in the case of westbound flights to avoid the strongest of the prevailing westerlies, and today's programmed track for BA298 gives the best route flight time from London to Chicago. The co-ordinates of the track are each cross-checked for accuracy against the flight plan. With so many aircraft crossing the Atlantic in the same direction at the same time on roughly parallel tracks a simple error in one

Fig 2:
Air Traffic Control flight plan.

Right:
At the 'Atlantic' desk in Operations the paperwork is spread before the crew. The other desks, 'Eastern'/'Southern' and UK/Europe, cover the remainder of the routes.

Fig 3:
Heathrow Terminal and stand layout.

co-ordinate could cause conflict. Airlines tend to schedule departures to similar destinations at much the same time, and, since all big jet aircraft prefer to operate at flight levels within the narrow 11,000ft band from 28,000 to 39,000ft, congestion often results, especially over such busy areas as the North Atlantic.

With the checking of the paperwork complete the crew is transported by car to the waiting aircraft at Terminal 1 on stand B27 on the north side of the airport. The British Airways' jumbo fleet is individually named, and flight BA298's aircraft today is *John Donne*, named after the famous 17th century English poet, preacher and prominent churchman. Crew refer to aircraft by the last two letters of the registration, in this case G-AWNJ, pronounced in the phonetic alphabet as 'november juliet'. At one time British Airways leased a 747 from Aer Lingus which flew regularly on the Chicago route. The aircraft registration was 'papa zulu', but was referred to affectionately by everyone as 'paddy zulu'. Before boarding 'november juliet' a quick check is made of the registration to ensure it is the correct flight. More

ATLANTIC

(HEATHROW) **LONDON**
RAMPS (CENTRAL)

18 JUL 83

than one crew in the world has prepared the wrong aircraft for service! The time is now 1340 with 35 minutes remaining until push back, and many checks and procedures are yet to be completed.

On board the Captain and First Officer commence their pre-flight checks while Flight Engineer Phil Roberts completes his walkround inspection. The aircraft, of course, is already prepared for service (apart from refuelling, catering, cargo loading, passenger boarding, etc!), but the crew are the last line of defence against errors made on the ground being carried into the air, and nothing is accepted without final check. The Flight Engineer's inspection is not intensive, but is more than just wings, two; engines, four, etc, and it is surprising the number of last minute requirements that are brought to light. The external check is known colloquially as 'kicking the tyres' and includes inspection of landing gear, check that the tyres are inflated and free from damage, chocks in position, ground locks removed, wing under surfaces free from fluid leaks and access panels closed, engines free from damage and leaks and access panels closed, flaps and flying controls

free from damage, and probes and sensors undamaged and covers removed. The maintenance log is normally first examined by the Captain to check aircraft condition, and any relevant defects that may affect performance. A dispatch deviation manual lists unacceptable defects which must be rectified before flight, but a number of minor malfunctions can be deferred for maintenance. On the Boeing 747, four generators — one to each engine — supply sufficient electricity to power a small town, and the miles of cables laid round the aircraft sometimes interact in ways which even the experts find baffling. On 'november juliet' the Captain notes from the maintenance log that any transmissions on number two high frequency radio (HF2) using a frequency of 13,000KHz result in the pressurisation outflow valves automatically driving open! Since pressurisation is supplied by engine-driven compressors pumping air via a cooling system into the cabin, and is controlled by outflow valves regulating exhausting air, any unscheduled opening of the outflow valves could catch the crew unawares. The situation, of course, sounds much more dramatic than is actually the

7

case, but it's certainly one to watch! It is not unusual for crews in such circumstances to place little bits of paper on equipment where a knob is not to be touched or a switch has to be thrown closed out of schedule, and on HF2 the Captain notices a small square of notepaper carefully attached to the offending radio. On it some wit has written the words 'ewes with care'!

It is also noted that number three engine is giving a slight vibration which can be felt through the thrust lever. All other indications are normal, but it's worth keeping an eye out for any further signs of trouble. An Australian newspaper once carried a report of a longhaul airliner whose Captain considered diverting to an en route airport because of an unidentified and persistent vibration which was causing concern. The source of the vibration was eventually discovered, after some time, to be a fitness enthusiast completing an hour's running on the spot in one of the toilets! Captain Edward Murray is satisfied with the condition of 'november juliet', but mentally notes the two defects listed for the flight. The dispatch deviation manual clearly indicates which defects are acceptable and which are not, so that the possibility of an aircraft being approved for flight in an unsatisfactory state does not arise. At any hint of an unsafe operation the crew would be the first to leave!

The Co-pilot switches the three inertial navigation system (INS) sets to 'align'. Each set operates quite independently in navigating the plane on its journey, and can be coupled to the autopilot to direct the jet along track at some suitable time after departure. The number of INS sets, ie three, is significant, as anyone with a watch on each wrist will tell you. If they're at different times it's impossible to tell which is correct. With three watches it can be reasonably assumed that any two indicating the same time are correct. (Similarly on board there are three compasses and three artificial horizons.) INS equipment is a 'hand me down' from the space age and is similar to systems used on the Apollo missions. A set of accelerometers positioned on a gyro-stabilised platform (electronically adjusted to maintain the local horizon) measures movement in all directions, including vertical, and computes the information to provide navigation data on position, track, drift, heading and speed, etc. The gyro platforms also provide stable horizontal reference for flight instruments. The navigation computer stores all global details and maintains an update of aircraft position at all times. On

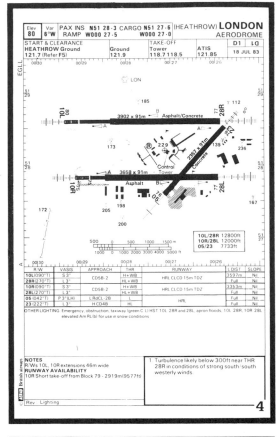

the ground at Heathrow, therefore, the computer knows where it is, although perhaps not always precisely. After long distances small errors creep in, and computed and actual positions may be slightly in error. The problem is overcome in what appears to be a delightfully simple manner but which, in essence, is highly complex. Using a single digit (ie one finger) the First Officer inserts the passenger terminal position for Heathrow (in degrees, minutes, and tenths of a minute) by using the INS keyboard. The required London airport position is 51° 28.3N; 000° 27.5'W, and is found on the first page of the aerodrome charts. In align mode the machine then compares computed and actual positions, adjusts itself to correct for error, and, believe it or not, by the basic process of detecting earth movement, recalculates true north. When considering that the complete process takes a maximum of only 13 minutes the feat is astounding!

The relevant paperwork is now distributed appropriately to each crew member, and the large number of books, manuals and documents carried on every flight, known collectively as the library, are checked by the Co-pilot against a list of requirements for the area of operation. As the INS gyros spin up, instrument failure flags retract and pre-flight instrument and equipment checks can be commenced. The procedure is known as a 'scan check', and each and every item is checked in sequence from memory. The scan commences at top right on the pilot's overhead panel, flows up and down through each piece of equipment, down across the autopilot and autothrottle switching on the glare shield, zig-zags across the pilot's centre panel and the Co-pilot's instrument panel (omitting the left instrument panel for checking by the Captain) and finally along the various items on the centre console. The checks are too numerous to mention individually but include oxygen check, radio switching, cockpit voice

Fig 4:
Heathrow Runway layout.

Fig 5:
Performance Manual Take Off summary.

Below:
Once on board the Flight Engineer commences his scan check. At the top of the picture the Flight Engineer's oxygen mask and smoke goggle compartment can be seen clearly.

| 02-03-12 / 12 JUN 81 / Issue 1 | B747 RTOW | PERFORMANCE MANUAL TAKE-OFF SUMMARY -7 | British airways |

LONDON HEATHROW — 10R — FLAP 10

Start Posn **FULL LENGTH**

A/D ELEV 80ft | R/W SLOPE .02UP

	TOR	ED	TOD(U)
	3658M	3658M	3647M
	12001ft	12001ft	11966ft

Temp °C	10kn TAIL	5kn TAIL	ZERO WIND	10kn HEAD	20kn HEAD	30kn HEAD
30	318.5 1.5	326.1 1.4	*333.3	0 *333.3	0 *333.3	0 *333.3
29	319.9	327.6 1.6	*335.4	*335.4	*335.4	*335.4
28	321.3	329.0 1.7	*337.6	*337.6	*337.6	*337.6
27	322.1 1.7	330.5	*339.0	0.2 *339.8	*339.8	*339.8
26	322.5 1.6	330.7	*339.0	0.4 *340.8	*340.8	*340.8
25	322.9	331.1	*339.4	0.3		
24	323.4	331.6	*339.9	0.2		
23	323.8	332.0	*340.3	0.1		
22	324.3	332.4	*340.7	0		
21	324.7	332.9 1.6	*340.8	0		
20	325.1	*333.3 1.5				
19	325.6	*333.7 1.4				
18	326.0	*334.1 1.3				
17	326.4	*334.6 1.2				
16	326.8	*335.0 1.2				
15	327.2	*335.4 1.1				
14	327.6	*335.8 1.0				
13	328.1	*336.2 0.9				
12	328.5	*336.6 0.8				
11	328.9	*337.1 0.7				
10	329.3	*337.5 0.7				
9	329.7	*337.9 0.6				
8	330.1	*338.3 0.5				
7	330.5	*338.7 0.4				
6	331.0	*339.1 0.3				
5	331.4	*339.4 0.3				
4	331.8	*339.8 0.2				
3	332.2	*340.1 0.1				
2	332.6	*340.5 0.1				
1	*333.0	*340.8 0				
0	*333.4 1.5					
-1	*333.8 1.4					
-2	*334.2 1.3					
-3	*334.6 1.2					
-4	*334.7 1.2					

V1 = CORRECTED VR −18 DRY / −28 WET

CORRECTIONS TO TABULATED SPEEDS – NIL

See Noise Abatement Table Opposite for NIGHT departures.

5

recorder test, window heat switching and check, warning lights test, ground proximity warning test, flight instrument checks, take-off configuration warning check and trim settings etc.

Once on board the Flight Engineer commences a similar scan check relevant to his instrument panel, checking and setting cabin altitude controls, checking fuel systems and monitoring refuelling, checking fire warning indicators, engine instrument display and safety equipment etc. He also examines the maintenance log and confers with the Captain and First Officer on any defects affecting performance. Meanwhile the Captain completes his pre-flight instrument check and begins to load the INS with latitude and longitude of positions en route. Take-off calculations are commenced by the Co-pilot, and the present Heathrow weather copied. Current weather conditions are transmitted continuously, and updated regularly, by the automatic terminal information service (ATIS), which is broadcast at Heathrow on a frequency of 121.85MHz. Each new transmission is progressively designated a letter of the alphabet, the present weather at 1345 GMT being 'november': wind 090° at 8kt, temperature +5°C/dew point +1°C, altimeter setting 1030 millibars, runway in use one zero right (10R), single runway operation (runway 10L/28R closed for inspection). From the take-off manual the maximum permitted take-off weight in today's conditions is extracted from a graph constructed from the details of runway 10R at Heathrow, and the weight noted on a take-off proforma. Five separate graphs refer to runway 10R alone — full length, noise abatement limits for night take-off on full length, take-off further down the runway at block 79, noise abatement limits for night take-off from block 79, and take-off from block 102 — so care must be taken in selecting the correct page. The graph is constructed with runway length and gradient in mind, and is entered with wind component and temperature. The maximum allowable take-off weight indicated provides sufficient obstacle clearance with one engine out for the first segments of the flight, ie initial climb, gear retraction, flap retraction and en route climb. Once the actual take-off weight is known the proforma can be completed with take-off speeds and engine power setting. Take-off is expected to be in excess of 300 tonnes (the maximum structural take-off weight being 332.9 tonnes), but the exact weight is not known until the loading is complete and the load sheet is presented to the

Fig 6:
Take off data.

Below:
The Captain loads the INS with the latitude and longitude of positions along route while the Co-pilot commences the take-off calculations. The pilots' oxygen masks can be seen above their heads. On the left, one of the spare seats, known as a jump seat, can be seen in the stowed position.

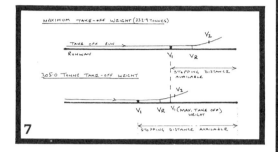

TAKE-OFF WEIGHT (TONNES)	V_R/V_2 (KNOTS)	TAKE-OFF ATTITUDE TARGET
330	167/172	14°
320	163/169	15°
310	159/166	15°
300	155/163	16°
290	151/159	16°
280	148/156	17°

(ACTUAL TAKE-OFF WEIGHT 305 TONNES)

8

7

Fig 7:
Take off speeds.

Fig 8:
Take off weight/speed chart.

Below:
Captain Edward Murray selects beacons for the standard instrument departure.

Captain for checking and signature about 10 minutes before departure. The stabiliser trim setting is also obtained from the load sheet. The Flight Engineer and First Officer cross-check from engine charts the maximum engine pressure ratio (EPR) available. The EPR is an indication of turbine discharge pressure to compressor inlet pressure and is a convenient method of displaying achieved power. The maximum EPR possible in today's conditions is seen to be 1.44 and is also noted on the take-off proforma. Since the take-off is at less than maximum weight, something less than maximum take-off power is sufficient, and what is known as a graduated power take-off can be considered.

The take-off speeds are designated 'V' for velocity and labelled V1, VR and V2. V1 is the go or no go decision speed. In the event of an emergency occurring before V1, sufficient runway is available for stopping, but if an emergency occurs after V1, the aircraft is committed to take-off. In fact, V1 is only critical at heavy take-off weights where abandoning at high speed and high weight, especially in restrictive conditions or from shorter runways, is a hazardous procedure. Overheating brakes and bursting tyres are likely and if swift action is not taken over-running of the runway length is a possibility. Since most take-offs are at something less than maximum weight, V1 becomes less critical with reduced weight. VR, the rotation speed, is the take-off speed (for that particular weight) at which the pilot pulls back on the control column and 'rotates' the aircraft to the nose up attitude required for lift off. At such point the jet becomes airborne. V2 is the safe climb out speed required in the event of losing an engine at the worst possible moment, ie just after V1. Normal climb out speed is V2+10. The take-off speeds of VR and V2 are extracted from a table against actual take-off weight of the aircraft, and since the take-off weight can vary by as much as 100 tonnes, the range of take-off speeds is wide. V1 is arranged to be a set number of knots (usually 10-20) below VR for all take-off weights, the knots reduction being indicated on the graph page of runway 10R in the take-off manual. On a wet runway aquaplaning can be caused when traction is impaired at speed by wedges of water building up between the tyres and runway surface, and a further reduction from VR in the region of 20kt is required to obtain V1. Standing water, slush or snow on the runway are a hazard in reducing acceleration and are only acceptable up to certain maximum thicknesses above which take-offs are not permitted. Where take-offs are possible in adverse conditions severe restrictions on the take-off weight are imposed which effectively reduces the take-off speeds. Such common knowledge would have been invaluable on a snow-blown day in Munich in 1958. At that time little or nothing was known of the effects of contaminated runways. On 6 February of that year at 3pm in the afternoon a plane carrying the Manchester United party endeavoured to take-off in a blizzard. At the third attempt the aircraft failed to get airborne and ran off the end of the runway. In the accident half the Manchester United team perished. The Captain was found negligent but some years later, with improvement in knowledge, was completely exonerated.

At this stage Captain Edward Murray is examining the standard instrument departure (SID) and is planning beacon selection and instrument settings for the required routeing. Although INS is engaged for most en route navigation, terminal area procedures are normally conducted using conventional navigation beacons. The two types of beacon in common use today are the NDB and VOR. The NDB — non-directional beacon — is a very basic piece of navigational equipment, and it's surprising, if not downright amazing, that modern jets still use such an antiquated aid!

The NDB transmits a signal on a fixed frequency, not unlike a broadcasting station, and equipment on board an aircraft, known as an automatic direction finder (ADF) detects the line of the incoming signal and points a needle in the direction of the beacon. The needle is superimposed on a compass rose to indicate magnetic bearing. The letters VOR stand for 'very high frequency omni-directional radio range'. This expanded version is carefully remembered by every student pilot for exam purposes, immediately forgotten afterwards, and forevermore, thankfully, remembered simply as the VOR. The beacon transmits bearing information by means of phase comparison. Radio beam transmissions 'radiate' from the beacon in all directions, like the spokes of a wheel, and not surprisingly are known as radials. On board the aircraft, bearing information is presented to the pilots by a vertical orange bar on the main compass system, known as a beam bar, which indicates the location of the required bearing, or radial, from the VOR. When the beam bar is central the jet is positioned on the selected radial.

The Captain is not certain of the departure route as clearances are not normally issued until engine start is requested, but an informed guess from the available details usually proves correct and beacon selection can be

Below:
The automatic direction finder (ADF), distance measuring equipment (DME) readouts above; main compass system to the right showing VOR beacon beam bar; radio transfer switches below.

Fig 9:
Departures Route chart.

accomplished at an early stage. Where a last minute runway change is announced because of change of wind direction etc, or an unexpected SID is allocated, take-off calculations, radio beacon selection, and rethinking of departure procedures may all have to be completed rapidly. Today the crew can expect a Daventry One Juliet (D1J) from runway 10R, which is outlined on the departure routes chart. This route sees the aircraft climb ahead to cross the 28L runway middle marker — positioned on the 135° radial from London VOR (morse identification L-O-N) at 2nm as indicated on the distance measuring equipment (DME) — then turn left to track 054° magnetic to pick up the London VOR 077° radial to Kilba at 11 DME from London. At Kilba it makes a left turn to track 022° magnetic to Brookmans Park NDB (morse identification B-P-K), and then left on to 311° magnetic to Daventry VOR (morse identification D-T-Y). There is also a requirement to cross Kilba above 3,000ft and to cross Brookmans Park level at 5,000ft. Further instructions to climb will be given from air traffic control on departure frequency 125.8MHz. Today's take-offs are easterly because of the wind direction, and this departure conveniently feeds 'november juliet' on to a northwesterly airway heading for the Atlantic, while at the same time keeping the jet clear of noise sensitive areas. To set up the instruments the London frequency of 113.6MHz is dialled on both VORs the radial 077° selected on the Captain's course indicator and 135° on the Co-pilot's. Brookmans Park NDB frequency of 328KHz is also selected on both ADF receivers, and the first height restriction of 5,000ft is set in the altitude select window.

The First Officer and Flight Engineer continue with the process of preparing the aircraft for flight while the Captain is now free to deal with problems as they arise. There may be a number of people who wish to liaise with him over technical problems, passengers missing, extra baggage, dangerous cargo, insufficient catering and a hundred other practical problems that all seem to appear just before departure. As time permits each crew member arranges the charts required for the journey and checks radio beacons identification, instrument settings and INS data. Seats, headsets and pilot's rudder pedals also require adjusting, and all this takes time. On completion of refuelling the Flight Engineer checks the figures with the refueller and passes the book forward to the Captain for final check and signature.

It is now approximately 10min to departure and with individual tasks complete the three crew members come together for the first time as a team to commence the 'engine start' check. The Co-pilot reads the check list to which each responds as items are called. The list includes a final check by all on the inserted INS present position and the latitude and longitude of the first three positions along route (known in crew jargon as way points), the checking and setting of radio

Below left:
The Co-pilot reads the checklist to which each responds as items are called. On the face of the building the bay number can be seen.

Below:
With a few minutes to spare the Captain takes the opportunity to give his briefing.

aids and instruments, and confirmation that such checks as oxygen, fuel etc, are complete. The 'engine start' check is halted at the item on take-off speeds while awaiting the arrival of the load sheet with the final take-off weight figure. At this point, with a few minutes to spare, the Captain takes the opportunity to give his briefing.

Captain 'Normal graduated power take-off. Departure is from one zero right. On crossing the two eight left middle marker, which is on the one three five radial from London at two DME, turn left to track zero five four magnetic and pick up the zero seven seven radial to Kilba. We've to cross Kilba above three thousand. At Kilba turn left to track zero two two magnetic to Brookmans Park. The first height restriction is five thousand feet and we've to cross Brookmans Park level. At Brookmans Park turn left on to three one one degrees into Daventry.

'The wind is about straight down the runway so there's no problem there. It's cold and damp today so I'll have engine anti-icing on as soon as the engines are started. As far as emergencies are concerned, if an emergency occurs before Vee one I'll call "stop", close the throttles, apply the brakes, manually select speed brakes and select idle reverse. If the emergency is an engine failure call me symmetrical engines available, and if the speed is above a hundred knots I'll select reverse power. If an emergency occurs after Vee one we'll take no action until the gear has been selected up, restate the emergency clearly, and I'll call for the appropriate drill. I'll fly the aircraft and handle the radio if you, Stan, and Phil, monitor each other with the drills upon my initiation. If we have to complete the full instrument departure I'll increase to the minimum manoeuvring speed of two hundred and sixty five knots for the turn to Daventry. Transition level is six thousand, and safety height in the area is two thousand three hundred.

It is now 1409 GMT, just six minutes to departure, and a dispatch clerk presents the load sheet to the Captain as he finishes his briefing. The Co-pilot notes the actual take-off weight of 305 tonnes and stabiliser trim setting of six divisions, and completes the take-off proforma while the Captain checks the loading. The weight difference between actual and maximum permitted allows a power reduction of 0.05 giving an engine pressure ratio setting per engine for take-off of 1.39. With the load sheet checked and

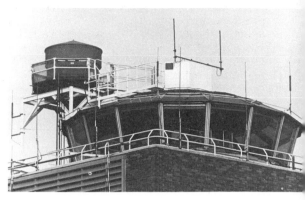

Above:
'Good afternoon, Speedbird Two Nine Eight cleared to start for Chicago'. The top of Heathrow Tower bristling with radio and radar antennae.

signed the clerk departs and the last door is heard to 'clunk' shut. The Captain and Co-pilot set bugs on their airspeed indicators (ASIs) against the speeds noted from the take-off proforma, and pointers on the engine gauges are set against the required EPR of 1.39. With take-off data set, thrust and start levers are checked closed and at cut off and the crew is ready for start. A slight delay now arises as some airmail and the last of the passengers' bags are loaded in the bulk cargo hold, then 'clearance' is called for start. The Co-pilot selects 121.7MHz on VHF radio box one.

First Officer R/T 'Clearance, good afternoon, Speedbird two nine eight, stand bravo two seven with information 'november', request start up.'

Clearance R/T 'Good afternoon Speedbird two nine eight, cleared to start for Chicago, Daventry one juliet departure, squawk five two three one. Call one two one decimal nine for push.'

The First Officer acknowledges the start and reads back the clearance, which is as anticipated. The squawk code given is a radar identification number and is selected on the transponder in preparation for departure. Seats and safety harnesses are checked locked and secure, the anti-collision beacon is switched on, and the Co-pilot requests clearance to start on intercom from the Ground Engineer. Parking brake is also checked and set and start pressure checked as sufficient. Engines are started in order 4, 1, 2

3, as No 4 engine powers No 4 hydraulic system which supplies main brakes. Jet engine start is a precise sequence and the Flight Engineer liaises closely with the Ground Engineer on intercom during the procedure. The Flight Engineer announces 'starting number four' and selects the ignition switch to ground start to turn the compressors. The Ground Engineer confirms on the intercom that N 1 (the fan) is beginning to turn while the Flight Engineer monitors N 2 (high pressure compressor) rotation and engine oil pressure rising from the gauges. At 22% N2 the Flight Engineer calls 'twenty two percent' and the Captain places No 4 start lever to idle while the First Officer starts the stop watch. Twenty seconds is the maximum time allowed for start up. Fuel is now pumping into the engine and the igniters are firing. Fuel flow is checked as normal. Five to ten seconds later the exhaust gas temperature (EGT) is seen to rise steadily, indicating light up. On occasions the light up process malfunctions and the EGT can be seen to climb rapidly towards the maximum of 650°C. A 'hot start' is called, and the start lever has to be placed quickly to cut off to shut off the fuel and the engine turned for 30 seconds for cooling before a second start can be attempted. The Flight Engineer calls 'thirty percent N two' and a check by all on No 4 engine gauges indicates the engine winding up normally. At 50% N2 the engine is self sustaining and the Flight Engineer releases the ignition switch. The EGT continues to rise, peaks, then settles back to idling level. Engine instruments are checked for normal operation and warning lights are checked extinguished. No 4 engine is now started. Jet engines are delicate pieces

Above:
The engine fan (the low pressure compressor referred to as N 1). To the right of the picture, below the wing, can be seen the canoe shaped fairings housing the flap-lowering mechanism.

Below:
Captain Murray now requests his First Officer to call for push back.

Bottom:
An engine roar is heard below the nose and the aircraft slowly begins to move backwards.

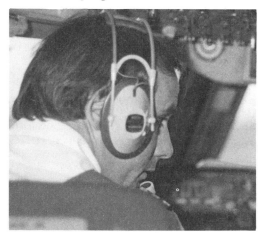

YU-AKB

of equipment to wind up and even a light tailwind blowing up the jet pipe can make starting difficult. When the engine is running, however, it becomes a roaring giant, each producing 48,000lb of static thrust at full power setting. Even at idle power a man can be drawn into the compressor within 8m of the intake and can be blown by jet blast within 45m of the tail pipe.

Captain Murray now requests his First Officer to call for push back. At all stands with movable covered walkways, which extend like fingers from the terminal, aircraft have to be parked nose in to the building and are required to be pushed back before taxi. Push back trucks are wide squat vehicles loaded with heavy weights which push aircraft back using tow bars connected to the nose wheel. If insufficient space is available in front of the aircraft they are also designed to fit below the belly and pull aircraft back from underneath. First Officer Stan Stewart switches the dual selector to 121.9MHz already dialled on VHF box one.

First Officer R/T 'Ground, good afternoon, Speedbird two nine eight, bravo twenty seven, request push back.'
Ground R/T 'Speedbird two nine eight, good afternoon, clear to push to face west.'
First Officer R/T 'Speedbird two nine eight, clear push, face west.'

The Captain confirms with the Ground Engineer on intercom that all ground equipment has been removed and is clear of the aircraft, that chocks have been removed from the nosewheel, and that the movable walkway has retracted.

Ground Engineer intercom 'Release brakes please.'
Captain 'Brakes are released.'

An engine roar is heard from the push back truck below the nose and the aircraft slowly begins to move backwards. The time is 1418 GMT, which is noted as an on time departure being just three minutes adrift. As the big jet eases tail first from the stand, the crew can see that more than the passengers have been waiting for this departure. Circling above is a group of seagulls which has been attracted by the activity and as the plane is pushed clear of the ramp they swoop to pick up scraps of food dropped by the caterers. The Ground Engineer remains on intercom and walks by the nose wheel with the aircraft. No 1 engine is started on push back. The remaining

engines cannot be started until push back is complete so the Captain takes the opportunity of the break to welcome the passengers on the flight. Today there are 250 on board, and although the maximum capacity is 404 the load factor is still over 60% which from a profit and loss view is on the right side of the break even point.

Captain PA 'Good afternoon ladies and gentlemen, Captain Murray speaking from the

Above:
The Ground Engineer calls for brakes to be set to park and engines number two and three are started. The Flight Engineer is seen selecting number two engine ignition switch to ground start. Across the glare shield, to the right of the Captain's shoulder, can be seen the autopilot switching.

Above right:
When all engines are running the engine start check is continued. A thumb carefully marks each item in turn.

Right:
The Captain advances the thrust levers with the right-hand, the left-hand on the tiller for steering.

flightdeck. Welcome aboard this British Airways Boeing seven four seven bound for Chicago. We'll shortly be taxying out to the runway and today we'll be taking off towards the east. After take-off we'll be turning left to head northwest across England, then up to the Mull of Kintyre in Scotland, from where we commence the Atlantic crossing. I'll speak to you again once we're airborne, in the meantime sit back and enjoy the flight, and if there's anything we can do to make the flight more comfortable please don't hesitate to ask.'

With the aircraft positioned for taxi, the Ground Engineer calls for brakes to be set to park and engines number two and three are started.

Starting procedures take a few minutes to complete, and when all engines are running the engine start check is continued. Start levers are checked at idle, stabiliser trim is checked and set, electrical, standby and galley power are all checked normal, air conditioning is checked and set, bleed valves are checked open, hydraulics are checked normal, door lights are checked out, the auxiliary power unit is checked stopped and brake pressure is checked normal. The Captain has a final word on the intercom with the Ground Engineer confirming the departure time of 1418 and requests the all clear signal on the left. The engine start check is now complete. The push back truck is detached and driven clear while the Ground Engineer disconnects his head set and stands safely to one side, arm raised vertically indicating all clear.

Captain 'Ask for taxi please.'
First Officer R/T 'Speedbird two nine eight, taxi.'

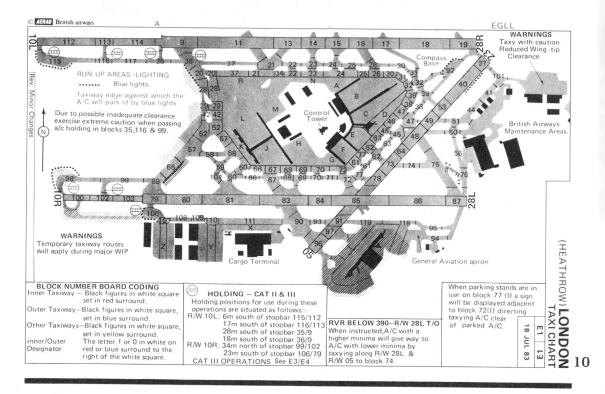

WARNINGS
Taxy with caution
Reduced Wing -tip
Clearance

RUN UP AREAS—LIGHTING
•••••• Blue lights.
Taxiway edge against which the
A/C will park lit by blue lights.

Due to possible inadequate clearance
exercise extreme caution when passing
a/c holding in blocks 35,116 & 99.

Compass
Base

Control
Tower

British Airways
Maintenance Areas.

Rev. Minor Changes

WARNINGS
Temporary taxiway routes
will apply during major WIP

Cargo Terminal

General Aviation apron

BLOCK NUMBER BOARD CODING
Inner Taxiway — Black figures in white square,
       set in red surround.
Outer Taxiway—Black figures in white square,
       set in blue surround.
Other Taxiways—Black figures in white square,
       set in yellow surround.
Inner/Outer   The letter 1 or 0 in white on
Designator   red or blue surround to the
       right of the white square.

HOLDING — CAT II & III
Holding positions for use during these
operations are situated as follows:-
R/W 10L: 6m south of stopbar 115/112
       17m south of stopbar 116/113
       28m south of stopbar 35/9
       18m south of stopbar 36/9
R/W 10R: 34m north of stopbar 99/102
       23m south of stopbar 106/79
CAT III OPERATIONS See E3/E4

RVR BELOW 390—R/W 28L T/O
When instructed,A/C with a
higher minima will give way to
A/C with lower minima by
taxying along R/W 28L &
R/W 05 to block 74.

When parking stands are in
use on block 77 (1) a sign
will be displayed adjacent
to block 72(1) directing
taxying A/C clear
of parked A/C.

18 JUL 83   E1   L3

(HEATHROW) **LONDON** TAXI CHART

10

Ground R/T 'Speedbird two nine eight, clear taxi behind the aircraft ahead. Follow him to one zero right.'

Along the taxiway a Lufthansa Boeing 737 is seen completing start up procedures. As this aircraft ahead moves off a quick check on either side of 'november juliet' confirms all is clear and the Captain releases the brakes and advances the thrust levers with the right hand, left hand on the tiller for steering. Engine whine is heard to rise as the engines spool up and the aircraft moves off under its own power. Although graceful in the air the Boeing 747 is cumbersome on the ground, and taxying the aircraft has been likened to driving a London bus down a narrow path whilst steering from the top deck. The time is now 1424 GMT and Speedbird 298 is on its way!

The 'before take-off' check is called for by the Captain as the aircraft taxis along the inner taxiway. (All check lists from now on are read by the Flight Engineer.) Take-off flaps are selected and checked at 10 degrees, speed brakes are checked down, flight controls are checked for operation and freedom of movement, flight instruments are checked, trim is checked set for take-off, annunciator panels are checked (all warning lights out),

and pressurisation is checked and set. The Captain also adds to his take-off briefing as deemed necessary. In the cabin, departure preparations and emergency briefings are complete, and Cabin Services Officer (CSO) Eddie Crockford reports to the Captain to confirm the cabin ready for take-off and that doors are set to 'automatic'. With 'automatic' mode selected the escape slides automatically deploy if the doors are opened in the event of an emergency evacuation being required.

Ground R/T 'Speedbird two nine eight continue following the Lufthansa seven three seven to one zero right. Call tower now one one eight decimal five.'
First Officer R/T 'Roger, Speedbird two nine eight, follow Lufthansa and call tower. Good day.'

The Co-pilot selects 118.5MHz.

First Officer R/T 'Tower, good afternoon, Speedbird two nine eight is with you.'
Tower R/T 'Thank you, Speedbird two nine eight. I'll call you back, you're number five.'

Lufthansa, not requiring the full runway length, holds at block 102, while Speedbird 298 passes behind and continues to the

Fig 10:
Heathrow taxi chart.

Top:
Lufthansa holds at block 102. An Iberian Boeing 727 lines up ready for take-off while Alitalia moves to the holding point.

Above:
Beyond the blast fence, only a few hundred metres away, a pretty cluster of quaint dwellings can be seen from the vantage of the flight deck, quite out of place in the environment of the airport.

Below:
Alitalia is also cleared for take-off.

holding point. A British Airways Tristar edges on to the runway and takes off. There are now two aircraft ahead, plus Lufthansa, awaiting take-off. On the right of the holding area an Alitalia DC-9 is seen standing clear of the taxiway resolving a technical problem. Beyond the blast fence, only a few hundred metres away, a pretty cluster of quaint dwellings can be seen from the vantage of the flightdeck, quite out of place in the environment of the airport. What sort of decibel level is heard in the lounges of these houses when a jet takes-off can hardly be imagined! An Iberian Boeing 727 bound for Madrid now

lines up ready for take-off, and Alitalia, problem solved, moves to the holding point. With the departure of Iberia, Alitalia is also cleared for take-off and Lufthansa prepares to line up from block 102.

Tower R/T 'Speedbird two nine eight, after the departing seven three seven line up and hold one zero right.'
First Officer R/T 'Speedbird two nine eight, after the seven three seven line up and hold.'

Two minutes later Lufthansa is cleared for take-off, and as the Boeing 737 rumbles down the runway Speedbird 298 moves into position at the threshold. The Captain calls for the completion of the before take-off check, and the Flight Engineer rapidly chimes the seat belt sign to announce take-off. Boost pumps are checked on, the fuel system is checked set, hydraulics and brakes are checked normal, air conditioning valves are checked off, ignition switches are positioned to flight start and, with 'november juliet' positioned straight on the runway, the body gear steering is switched off. A final check from memory using a simple mnemonic is made by each to confirm all is well. Speedbird 298 is now ready for take-off and holds on the runway awaiting clearance.

In spite of the size of today's large jets, advantage is still taken of prevailing winds and, where possible, aircraft land and take-off into wind. At heavy weight take-offs, even slight changes in the wind direction or speed can be critical. In today's conditions the wind of 090° at 8kt is blowing more or less down the runway resulting in a head wind com-

Top:
Two minutes later Lufthansa is cleared for take-off and Speedbird 298 moves into position at the threshold of 10R.

Above:
Speedbird 298 is now ready for take-off and holds on the runway awaiting clearance. (Pilot's seats move aft and then to the side on tracks to allow easier access from the centre of the flight deck. During take-off and landing the seat must be locked within the first 7in of track for correct pilot positioning at controls.)

Above right:
Speedbird 298 is 'cleared for take-off'. (The Flight Engineer's seat swivels to the right to face the instrument panel, but must be forward or 50° right of forward, during take-off and landing.)

Right:
The Flight Engineer leans forward and finely adjusts each thrust lever to the precise engine pressure ratio setting.

20

ponent of 8kt and nil cross wind. Rotation speed is 159kt relative to the air, so the aircraft will become airborne at a ground speed of 151kt (159-8), which can make a significant difference at heavy take-off weights, especially where the airport is hot and high (eg the mile high city of Denver in Colorado). At rotation the airspeed indicator will, of course, read 159kt. The Boeing 747 can take-off and land with a tail wind (depending on the runway length and aircraft weight) but the maximum acceptable tail wind strength is only 10kt.

The Lufthansa 737 is now a few minutes ahead on its climb and Speedbird 298 is given clearance for take-off.

Tower R/T 'Speedbird two nine eight cleared for take-off. Wind zero nine zero at eight.'
First Officer R/T 'Speedbird two nine eight, cleared for take-off'.

The Captain's right hand is on the throttles, the left hand on the steering tiller, and feet on the rudder pedals with the aircraft being held on the toe brakes. The First Officer holds the control column forward and the Flight Engineer positions between the two pilots, slightly aft, ready to monitor power. The Captain calls 'standby for take-off'. On brake release the Captain stands the thrust levers up to the vertical position and elapsed time is started on the clocks. Engine gauges are seen to wind up, and as the engines stabilise the Captain advances the throttles close to the required power setting.

Captain 'Set graduated power.'

The Flight Engineer leans forward and finely adjusts each thrust lever to the precise engine pressure ratio setting. The acceleration speed is rapid with the aircraft gaining 3-5kt/sec. As the airspeed indicators become effective the needles are seen to move on both the Captain's and First Officer's instruments and the Co-pilot calls 'airspeed building'. At 80kt the rudder becomes more effective and at the call of 'eighty knots' from the Co-pilot the Captain transfers his left hand to the control column and continues to steer with the pedals.

Captain 'I have the control column.'
First Officer 'Your control.'

Speeding down the runway now the aircraft is maintained on the centre line by delicate movements of the rudder. The use of the rudder at this stage in guiding the aircraft on the take-off run, and also on the roll out after landing, is the only time at which the rudder is employed in a similar manner as on a ship. During asymmetric flight, with one engine out, rudder is also applied to maintain the aircraft straight, but all turns in flight are effected by aileron control. The Captain's right hand is poised on the throttles ready to close them in the event of an abandoned take-off while the left hand holds the control column forward. The First Officer and Flight Engineer scan instruments and monitor progress. Abandoning take-off now could be a hazardous procedure and is only initiated by a major emergency such as an engine failure. When a serious emergency arises before V1 the Captain immediately calls 'stop', closes the throttles, deploys the speed brakes, selects reverse thrust, and at the same time applies full brakes. Taking-off at maximum weight the V1 speed can be close to 150kt and stopping a large mass like the jumbo at such a speed generates enormous brake heat energy. The brakes almost certainly overheat and require hours to cool. The tyres, in fact, are fitted with fusible plugs which melt at 350°F, and are designed to prevent tyre explosions at high temperatures.

At 141kt the Co-pilot calls 'Vee one'. The aircraft is now committed to take-off and the Captain moves his right hand from the thrust levers to the control column, the Flight Engineer assuming control of the engines. Acceleration is still rapid. An engine failure now could result in a marked swing which would have to be quickly corrected by rudder. Also, with loss of power from one engine the aircraft would have to be held on the runway a little longer until rotate speed had been achieved. However, no other action would be taken at this stage as engine failure drills are not commenced until the jet is safely airborne and the gear has been selected up.

As the speed reaches 159kt the Co-pilot calls 'rotate'. The Captain pulls steadily backwards on the control column at just the right rate until 15° nose up attitude is reached on the artificial horizon and the aircraft is held in this position. The take-off run is about 40sec and at time 1438 Speedbird 298 lifts off and is airborne!

The Captain is now flying on instruments irrespective of the weather. 'Vee two' is called almost immediately by the First Officer, and with positive rate of climb indication, gear is selected up on the Captain's command. At 175kts (V2+10) the speed is held by adjusting the rate of climb and the aircraft buffets in the wind as it encounters some light low-level turbulence. The cloud layer can be seen above and visibility is poor in the hazy conditions. Approaching 500ft the flashing amber of the 28L middle marker is seen on the panel and as the beam bar passes through the First Officer's compass centre line the Captain turns the jet to track 054° magnetic, adjusting the heading accordingly to allow for drift as indicated on the INS. The Co-pilot now selects the 077° radial on his VOR course indicator to match that already set on the Captain's side.

Tower R/T 'Speedbird two nine eight, call Departure one two five decimal eight.'
First Officer R/T 'Speedbird two nine eight, good day.'

125.8MHz is selected

Left:
As the speed reaches 159kt the Co-pilot calls 'rotate'.

Below left:
The Captain pulls back steadily on the control column at just the right rate . . . Note the nosewheel lifting.

Above:
With positive rate of climb indication the gear is selected up on the Captain's command. Note the landing gear doors open first, increasing drag, before retraction commences. The leading edge flaps can also be clearly seen extended from the front of the wings.

First Officer R/T 'Good afternoon Departure, Speedbird two nine eight is passing one thousand two hundred.'
Departure R/T 'Good afternoon, Speedbird two nine eight, maintain five thousand on reaching.'

At 1,500ft the Co-pilot calls the height and the Captain requests climb power. The throttles are eased back by the Flight Engineer to the climb power setting shown on the indicator, and the Captain reduces the climb by lowering the nose to about 10°-12° nose up attitude to allow for power reduction. Flight directors are switched on at this point and the pitch and heading bars are set as required and used to help indicate the flight path as the Captain maintains handling control of the aircraft. The nose is now lowered a little more to gain

speed for flap retraction. As the speed edges past 205kt and increasing the Captain calls for 5° flap. The speed is checked by the First Officer and 5° flap selected with the Flight Engineer monitoring operations.

First Officer 'Flap five set.'

The aircraft is above 2,000ft now, barely climbing, and is still accelerating. Just above 225kt the Captain calls for flap 1°. After a further check of the speed the First Officer selects flap 1°, and as the trailing edge flaps retract from 5° to 1°, half the leading edge flaps also come in automatically. With flaps extended beyond 1° a maximum speed limit of 240kt applies and the Captain is required to maintain the speed within the narrow 15kt band between the minimum and maximum speeds of 225 and 240kt by climbing the aircraft until 1° flap is set and acceleration can be continued. 'Beam bar active' is called by the Co-pilot and the Captain gently turns the aircraft right to track the 077° radial while also concentrating on flap retraction.

First Officer 'Flap one set.'

At 3,200ft the jet passes over Kilba and the Captain turns left to track 022° magnetic to Brookmans Park using the ADF needles pointing to the beacon. Acceleration is recommenced and the Captain calls, 'Flaps in please.' Speed is checked above 245kt and the First Officer selects flap zero. Meanwhile the remainder of the leading edge flaps retract automatically.

First Officer 'Flaps are in.'

The flight is smooth now as the Captain maintains a speed of 250kt, the maximum allowable in the area below 10,000ft, although requests can be made for higher for operational requirements, and speed mode is engaged on the flight director.

First Officer 'One to go.'

The jet passes 4,000ft with 1,000 to go to the first cleared altitude.

Captain 'After take-off check please.'

The Flight Engineer commences the after take-off check. In light cloud the plane is rapidly climbing towards 5,000ft and the Captain eases back on the power to gently capture the height while maintaining 250kt. As Speedbird 298 is just settling at 5,000ft, one of 'Murphy's laws' applies: departure clears the jet to 6,000ft. The Captain calls for climb power and eases the aircraft once more into the climb. Almost immediately Departure control calls back.

Departure R/T 'Speedbird two nine eight recleared level one two zero. Call London now, one three four decimal seven five.'

134.75MHz is selected.

First Officer R/T 'London, good afternoon, Speedbird two nine eight out of five for level one two zero.'

London R/T 'Good afternoon Speedbird two nine eight, roger, recleared now present position direct Pole Hill. No speed restriction.'

Pole Hill position is already inserted in the INS in way point 4, and the Captain keys 0-4 on the INS to obtain required track. The aircraft is turned on to track and the nose lowered to increase speed. As a back up the First Officer also selects and identifies the Pole Hill frequency of 112.1MHz on both VORs. Passing 6,000ft, the transition altitude, the standard pressure setting of 1,013.2 millibars is set on both altimeters. All heights are now given in terms of flight level, ie 12,000ft is equivalent to flight level 120.

Meanwhile the Flight Engineer is completing the after take-off check. Probe heat is checked on, ignition and engine anti-icing are left on, cabin signs are switched off, outboard landing lights are left on until 10,000ft as a

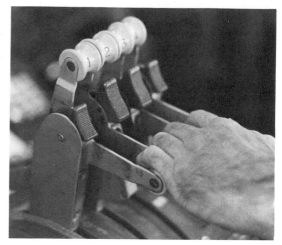

Above:
The throttles are eased back by the Flight Engineer to the climb power setting. Engines are numbered 1 to 4 from left to right as shown by the thrust levers. The top knobs are used by the pilots while the palm switches between are used to initiate an automatic 'go-around'. The levers protruding forward are used for reverse thrust selection.

Fig 11:
Radio Navigation chart.

'see and be seen' precaution, landing gear is checked up and the lever confirmed in off position, all lights out, pack valves are checked all on, air conditioning and fuel systems are checked, and flaps are checked in, all lights out. Just above 7,000ft Speedbird 298 breaks through the light cloud layer into a clear blue shining sky.

Flight Engineer 'Switching off the engine anti-icing now, Captain.'

Settled in the climb at the required speed of 320kt, the Captain engages the autopilot and selects INS navigation and speed mode switch. The aircraft is now under control of the autopilot with the INS navigating on a direct track to Pole Hill thus leaving the Captain more free to monitor and manage the operation of the flight. At level 120 the autopilot will automatically capture the height which is already set in the altitude select window. Passing 10,000ft the First Officer calls 'altimeter check', and all acknowledge 'passing one zero zero for level one two zero, standard set'. The Flight Engineer leans forward and switches off the outboard landing lights. Control calls now and instructs Speedbird 298 to contact London on

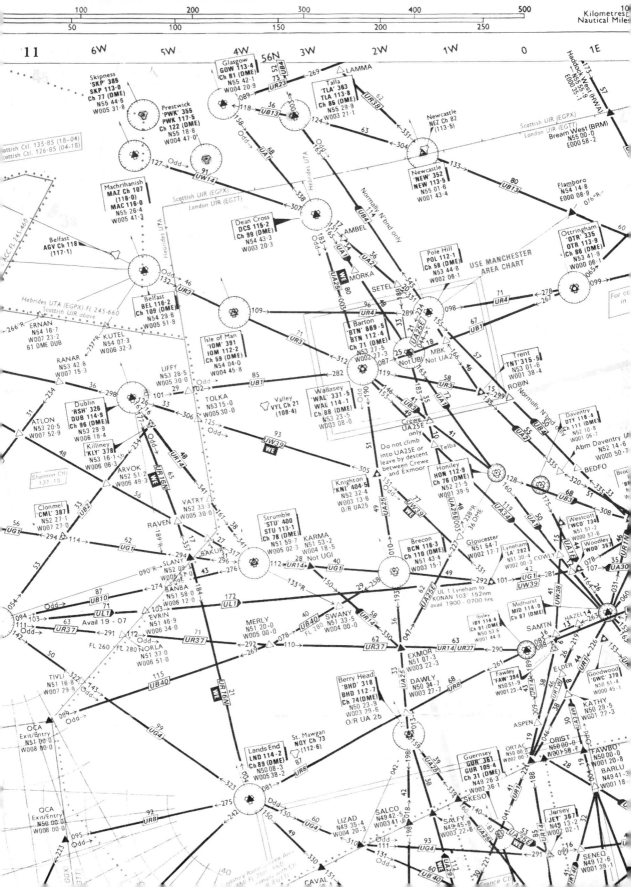

131.05MHz and the Co-pilot establishes contact.

London R/T 'Good afternoon, Speedbird two nine eight. Recleared level two six zero now, and also direct Dean Cross.'

Dean Cross is a VOR beacon on the north coast of Cumbria, just west of Carlisle, so the direct routeing is useful and should save both time and fuel. Directly below a thin cloud cover blankets the Midlands; beneath the edge, as it clears, can be seen Manchester, and in the distance, the hills of the Pennines. At a number of points on the layer small cumulus clouds protrude like mushroom caps from the stratus and mark the positions of power stations where the warm air rises above the plants to make their own cloud formations. Passing 20,000ft the second 'altimeter check' is called and the INS indicates 150nm to Dean Cross. The aircraft has been airborne for just 15min.

During the climb the crew sum leg times on each flight log to obtain estimated times at all positions en route to Chicago. The Co-pilot notes the estimate for Machrihanish as 1527 and 56°N 10°W, the first position on the North Atlantic track, as 1546. Although flight plans are submitted for the entire route it is not always possible for aircraft to reach Atlantic entry points at estimated times and flights are handled as they arrive. A combined Shannon and Prestwick control known as Shanwick supervises the entire eastern Atlantic out to 30° west and it's a require-

ment to call Shanwick for confirmation of the routeing as early as possible. The Captain suggests the Co-pilot calls Shanwick now while he monitors London on VHF box one. 127.65MHz is selected on VHF2 and the First Officer calls Shanwick control.

First Officer R/T 'Shanwick, good afternoon, Speedbird two nine eight.'
Shanwick R/T 'Speedbird two nine eight, Shanwick, good afternoon, go ahead.'
First Officer R/T 'Speedbird two nine eight, airborne out of Heathrow at one four three eight, estimating Machrihanish at one five two seven and five six north one zero west at one five four six. Request Atlantic routeing as filed at flight level three five zero, mach decimal eight four.'
Shanwick R/T 'Roger Speedbird two nine eight, standby.'

The First Officer maintains a listening watch on 127.65MHz as the flight details and estimates are fed to the oceanic computer for analysis. Meanwhile on VHF1 London calls and clears Speedbird 298 to continue climb to flight level 280. The Captain acknowledges and selects 28,000ft on the altitude select which is confirmed by the Flight Engineer.

Shanwick R/T 'Speedbird two nine eight, Shanwick, your oceanic.'

The First Officer signals the Flight Engineer to monitor the clearance with him as it is

Left:
Settled in the climb at the required speed of 320kt the Captain engages the autopilot and checks the routeing from the flight logs.

Below:
Approaching 20,000ft the Flight Engineer adjusts the climb power setting.

imperative that two listen to such important instructions.

First Officer R/T 'Speedbird two nine eight, go ahead.'
Shanwick R/T 'Shanwick clears Speedbird two nine eight to Chicago via Machrihanish, five six north one zero west, five seven north two zero west, five eight north four zero west, five eight north five zero west, Prawn, Schefferville, flight level three five zero mach decimal eight four from five six north one zero west.'

The First Officer reads back the clearance precisely.

Shanwick R/T 'That's affirmative Speedbird two nine eight. Continue now with domestic. Good day.'
First Officer 'I'm back on VHF one now Captain. We've got the route as requested at flight level three five zero.'

The aircraft levels off at 280 over Morecambe Bay and a click is heard as green lights glow indicating positive height capture by the autopilot.

First Officer R/T 'London Speedbird two nine eight now level two eight zero.'
London R/T 'Roger Speedbird two nine eight. Call Scottish now one three five decimal eight five.'

A quick change of frequency is made.

First Officer R/T 'Scottish, good afternoon, Speedbird two nine eight. We have our oceanic, as filed at flight level three five zero.'
Scottish R/T 'Thank you Speedbird two nine eight, now cleared direct fifty-six north ten west, with your estimate please, and recleared level three five zero.'

56°N 10°W is on way point seven, and with 0-7 keyed on the INS the aircraft turns automatically on the direct routeing. The Captain turns to the Flight Engineer who has the same thought in mind and is quickly checking graphs.

Flight Engineer 'We're too heavy for three five zero at the moment.'

The Captain turns to the First Officer.

Captain 'Ask him if three three zero is available and say we'd like to maintain that for as long as possible.'

The Co-pilot relays the request to Scottish.

Scottish R/T 'OK Speedbird two nine eight, recleared level three three zero now and cleared to cross five six north ten west at three five zero.'

Climb power is requested and by adjustment of autopilot controls the Captain eases Speedbird 298 gently into the climb. The INS shows the time to 10°W as 34min and the Co-pilot passes to Scottish the estimate for 56°N 10°W as 1548 GMT. Far below the cloud cover has dispersed and as Morecambe Bay slips under the nose the view from the flight deck in the excellent visibility is quite spectacular. Ahead can be seen the Solway Firth and beyond the Southern Uplands of Scotland, with the Galloway coast clearly defined. On the right the snow-covered Pennines simmer in the sunshine while on the left the Isle of Man basks lazily in the Irish Sea. Atlases are extracted from briefcases as the crew pick out points of interest on the ground while monitoring the climb and the flight's progress.

Over the Solway Firth Speedbird 298 levels off at 330. As the speed builds up the Flight Engineer eases back on the thrust levers and sets the required power of 1.42 EPR to maintain a speed of Mach 0.84 on the Machmeter. At normal cruise levels the air is too thin to use the standard airspeed indicator and cruise speeds are set relative to the speed of sound using the Machmeter. The speed of sound, however, does not remain constant, but varies with temperature — for example it's about 660kt at sea level and about 590kt at 30,000ft. For simplification the Austrian physicist Ernst Mach designated the numerical value of 1.0 as the speed of sound in any conditions. Concorde, for example, cruises at Mach 2.0, twice the speed of sound for the particular flying conditions of that environment. Today, at 33,000ft, Speedbird 298 is cruising at Mach 0.84, or, in other words, at 84% of the speed of sound at that level. Two other speeds are important. At high speed shock waves form on the wings causing buffet, and at low speed the onset of the stall has a similar effect. Speed, therefore, has to be monitored frequently by the Flight Engineer and adjusted by setting the thrust levers to maintain the speed constant and to keep the speed within limits. Required speed is extracted from a table of height against weight, the all up weight of the aircraft being taken from an indicator set before departure which runs down as fuel is consumed.

The climb to 330 has taken 36min and covered 190nm. Speedbird 298 is now settled in the cruise heading 310° magnetic over Stranraer with a magnificent panorama unfolding for the crew. Rarely does the weather in the United Kingdom afford such a beautiful sight and the Captain makes full use

Above:
The Captain suggests the Co-pilot call Shanwick now while he monitors London on VHF box one.

Below:
The Captain turns to the Flight Engineer who has the same thought in mind and is quickly checking graphs. The weight of the aircraft is checked against the available flight level — the heavier the aircraft the lower the cruise height.

Below right:
Over the Solway Firth Speedbird 298 levels off at 330 and, as the speed builds up the Flight Engineer eases back on the thrust levers to set the required power.

of the PA in outlining the sights as the flight progresses. It is sometimes difficult to judge the extent of information required by passengers as experienced travellers usually prefer the bare minimum and 'first timers' want to hear it all. Today, however, is an exception and the Captain's informed observations are much appreciated by all on board. On the right the coastline of Scotland stretches up towards the Firth of Clyde, the rock of Ailsa Craig bird sanctuary is seen off Girvan, and 40 miles away the black tarmac runway at Prestwick airport stands out clearly. The Mull of Kintyre lies ahead and Ireland and Belfast Lough come into view on the left.

With the North Atlantic route confirmed track co-ordinates are now keyed into the INS using way points of positions already passed. These track positions are imaginary places as there is actually nothing there — they are simply convenient co-ordinates — although progress reports are radioed at these points along the way. Today five North Atlantic westbound tracks are lettered from A to E, (eastbound tracks are V, W, X, Y, Z), but all lie to the south and are unsuitable for the Chicago routeing. The INS flies a great circle track, which is the shortest distance between points, but may not be the quickest because of the prevailing westerly winds blowing against traffic from Europe to the States,

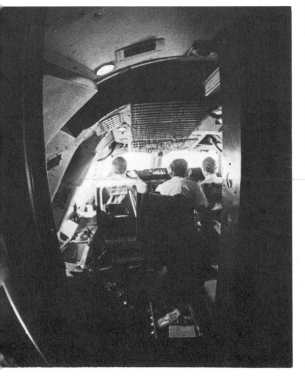

which are sometimes very strong. The computer, therefore, plots a route giving fastest time, which is normally a compromise between great circle track and best wind. This afternoon the winds are much lighter than normal and do not pose a problem. Since the published tracks are too far south for Speedbird 298 the computer has produced a 'composite' track as a 'one off' routeing for London-Chicago. The routeing for today's New York flight, for example, lies further south, and is planned on one of the published tracks. Aircraft, of course, arrive from all over Europe to only five entry points for these tracks, and a flight's first choice may not always be available. The paperwork on board, unfortunately, is only for the requested routeing, and if second preference is allocated images of the First Officer resembling a one-armed paper hangar as he rewrites by hand the entire North Atlantic route are not unfounded!

The Mull of Kintyre slips by on the right followed by the islands of Islay and Jura standing proud in the bright light against the dark sea. On the horizon the snow-capped Grampian Mountains frame the skyline. On the left the coast of Ireland and Loch Foyle can clearly be seen. Minutes later thin wisps of cloud stream past the flight deck windows and in a moment a curtain descends and the plane is enveloped in thin cloud. The show is over! Meanwhile in the cabin lunch is being served. A young boy on board in his early teens has a birthday today, and a few days before British Airways was informed by his family of the coming event. Imagine his surprise when, during the meal, Cabin Services Officer Eddie Crockford presents him with a birthday cake. On the flightdeck the crew make do with a flask of tea and some biscuits and will not eat until much later when the cabin crew are free. In the air the passengers definitely come first.

Approaching ten west the aircraft is once again eased into the climb for level 350.

First Officer R/T 'Scottish, Speedbird two nine eight leaving level three three zero for level three three five zero, will call reaching.'

The first North Atlantic position report of 56°N 10°W is crossed by 'november juliet' at 1546 GMT level at 350, and this information is relayed to Scottish.

Scottish R/T 'Thank you Speedbird two nine eight. Call Shanwick now on five six four nine, secondary eight eight seven nine.'

The First Officer selects 5,649KHz on HF1, the long distance radio which will be used right across the Atlantic until VHF contact is once again established on the far shore. A secondary frequency of 8,879KHz is also given in case atmospherics distort the primary frequency. In the use of HF radio clarity and formality are the order of the day as conditions, on occasions, can make transmissions difficult and position reports on the North Atlantic are always given in a strict format.

First Officer R/T 'Shanwick, Speedbird two nine eight, position.'
Shanwick R/T 'Speedbird two nine eight, go ahead.'
First Officer R/T 'Shanwick, Speedbird two nine eight, five six north one zero west at one five four six, level three five zero, estimating five seven north two zero west at one six two seven, five eight north three zero west next. Temperature minus five eight degrees celsius, wind zero five zero at one five. Selcal check please, bravo delta hotel lima.'

Selcal is a call system whereby selection of a four-letter code at control centre activates a chime on the flightdeck, accompanied by flashing yellow lights, which alerts crews that contact is being attempted, not unlike the ringing of a telephone. After HF communication has been established and selcal checked, it is not necessary to maintain a listening watch and headsets can be removed for comfort. The emergency frequency of 121.5MHz is always set on one VHF box and can be monitored via the flightdeck speaker.

The Captain now lifts the handset to speak to the passengers.

Captain PA 'Good afternoon ladies and gentlemen, Captain Murray speaking once again from the flightdeck. I trust you're comfortable and enjoying the flight. We're now lying one hundred and fifty miles west of Scotland at thirty five thousand feet over the Atlantic. Flight time remaining is about $6\frac{1}{2}$ hours, and we're estimating arrival at the gate in Chicago on schedule at four forty five local time in the afternoon. For those of you who would like to set your watches the time in Chicago is six hours behind London, and at the moment it is ten o'clock in the morning. The winds on the Atlantic are lighter than normal today and with some luck we may be a few minutes early. The Atlantic route takes us up to fifty eight north at thirty west, the mid-point of the crossing. We then pass about

Above:
The attitude director indicator (ADI) or more simply, artificial horizon, showing level flight. The light area represents the sky, the dark the earth and the horizontal line the horizon. The model aircraft sits at 2° nose up with the crossed bars of the flight detector system indicating attitude and heading required to maintain height and track. On the right is the radio altimeter, and on the left the airspeed indicator, with the bugs used to mark speeds on take-off and landing bunched at the top.

Below:
Club Class passengers in the upper deck lounge behind the flight deck relax for the flight ahead. Those with a window seat enjoy the view described by the Captain.

one hundred and twenty miles south of Greenland before making land fall close to the small town of Nain on the Labrador coast of Canada. The route then takes us southwest bound right across Canada, passing over Labrador, Quebec and Ontario, down to the Great Lakes, where we cross into the States, and then on to Chicago. The en route weather has been reported as good and the forecast for Chicago is fresh winds, partly cloudy, with the possibility of light snow showers. I'll speak to you again at the far side of the Atlantic, and in the meantime, I'll wish you all a pleasant trip.'

The thin cloud now clears and Speedbird 298 breaks out into a bright blue sky with a heavy layer of cloud far below blanketing the sea. In the meantime the Flight Engineer completes his first fuel check and passes the details forward to the Captain for inspection. The fuel used is summed from integrators and compared with fuel still in the tanks as indicated by the gauges in kilogrammes. The weight of the fuel on board is also added to the known zero fuel weight to check the indicated all up weight. Fuel to destination is calculated and subtracted from the fuel in tanks to obtain the fuel available on arrival. A minimum fuel figure at destination is, obviously, required in case of diversion caused by bad weather, and in adverse conditions of strong head winds or low flight altitude, reserves may be reduced to a level at which an en route landing becomes necessary. Fuel condition, therefore, is monitored throughout the flight and fuel checks are conducted at regular intervals. The figures at 10°W show 88.4 tonnes of fuel remaining with 69.3 tonnes required to destination, leaving 19.1 tonnes diversion fuel available. A quick check of the fuel flight plan shows 18.9 tonnes required for diversion and contingency so at this stage Speedbird 298 is performing just that little bit better than planned. Total fuel consumption is 12.0 tonnes/hr (ie each engine is gulping three tonnes/hr) and is equal to almost one gallon of kerosene being burned every second! At take-off, with full power set, fuel consumption can soar to 30 tonnes/hr, although, of course, such levels are only sustained for short periods.

Modern engines such as those on the Boeing 747 are known as fan jets, the first or N1 compressor being similar to a circular fan consisting mainly of a giant single ring of large blades, not unlike a many bladed propellor with the tips cut off. And, indeed, the fan is more like a propellor than a compressor, delivering 77% of the thrust of the complete engine. Much fan air is arranged to bypass the main engine core to improve propulsive efficiency and exhausts straight to the atmosphere. An added advantage of the fan jet is the reduction in noise. Jet noise is due to the shear effect of a high speed jet cutting the atmosphere. On the fan jet the by-passed air shrouds the jet core, lessening the shear and reducing the noise. Aircraft noise is measured in perceived noise decibels (PNdB) which is a measure of the type as well as the level of noise. The Boeing 747 scores about 107 PNdB at heavy weight take-offs and landings.

Approaching 20°W the INS way points are re-checked for the next leg and at 1627 GMT the aircraft automatically turns to steer the great circle track towards 30°W. The time at 20°W and estimate for 58°N 30°W are noted and the co-pilot transmits on HF the position report and spot wind and temperature to Shanwick. The Flight Engineer completes the second fuel check and the Captain notes at destination the fuel available is still improving on planned requirements.

With Speedbird 298 settled on the North Atlantic route some of the pressure is now off the flight crew and they can relax a bit for the three-hour crossing which lies ahead. In spite of the workload being reduced in the cruise, however, there is still a number of tasks required over and above the normal flight management and monitoring duties which keep crews alert. Navigation has tas to be re-checked at reporting points, way points have to be updated accordingly, speed monitored continuously, flight logs kept up to date, position reports radioed, en route wind and temperature noted, destination and diversion aircraft weather copied regularly, en route weather lookout and weather radar monitoring, etc. The Flight Engineer is also required to update speed and power requirements as weight reduces with fuel consumption, complete regular fuel checks which are passed to the Captain for analysis, and to keep instrument monitoring logs up to date. All emergency drills, though, can be accomplished by only two crew members, and one may be allowed freedom to stretch his legs for a few minutes from time to time.

The sky is still bright and clear but miles below a thick layer of cloud continues to mask the ocean. Approaching the middle of the Atlantic, pilots are in a privileged position to view the weather which will reach England on the following day. The heavy stratus seen moving westwards will no doubt result in a dull and perhaps drizzly day, but there is little sign of any frontal systems which normally ply their way across the Atlantic bringing characteristically showery weather to the shores of Britain. The North Atlantic region is, meteorologically, an area of particular interest and weather patterns found in the vicinity are worthy of discussion.

When considering, in general terms, geographical influence on weather, it can be seen that the factor most affecting temperature is latitude, the earth, obviously, being cold at the Poles and hot at the equator. This varying heating effect of the sun at different latitudes results in distinct characteristics of air being formed in bands around the world. The property of air within each band depends primarily on the temperature and humidity; the warmer the air the greater its capacity to hold moisture. Divisions between the bands of air of different characteristics is quite defined, although the transition zone may be several miles wide. On the northern part of the Atlantic lies the Polar air band and to the south the Tropical air band, with the transition zone between them lying across the North Atlantic resulting in the frequently changeable weather activity of the region.

Properties of air within a principal air band may vary according to the differing moisture content, but when air of more or less the same characteristics covers a large area, perhaps hundreds or even thousands of miles across, it is called an air mass. Local air masses from adjacent principal air bands infringe upon each other's territories forming wave-like zones of conflict between the air bands. Two Norwegian meteorologists studying this phenomenon during World War 1 aptly named the lines of limit of advance of air masses as fronts. The transition zone over the North Atlantic where the Polar and Tropical air bands meet is known as the Polar front, and is an area of intense frontal activity. The interaction between opposing air masses results in a fragmented wave-like pattern of frontal sections being formed, stretching across the Atlantic in family groups from Florida to SW England in the winter and from Newfoundland to the Faroe Islands in the summer, drifting continuously eastward towards Europe and Scandinavia on the prevailing westerly winds. The fronts are often areas of large cloud formations, and the lines of cloud marking the extent of the fronts can frequently be seen from the flightdeck. The fronts can bring much rain and are directly responsible for the cloudy, showery weather prevalent in the United Kingdom. They can travel at 30-40kt and can cover almost 1,000nm in one day. Weather seen in the middle of the Atlantic, therefore, often reaches Europe the next day, and on such occasions crews on westbound flights to the States have a grandstand view of tomorrow's weather in the United Kingdom.

The vertical extent of cloud formations is also influenced by the variable heating effect

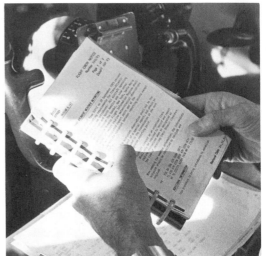

Top:
The vertical speed indicator shows the aircraft level at 35,000ft. Bottom left is the main compass system with the ground speed indicating 479kt.

Above:
Before the first HF position report the First Officer checks the latest Atlantic weather reporting procedures.

Above right:
The Captain now lifts the hand-set to speak to the passengers.

Fig 12:
Speedbird 298 Atlantic route.

of the sun with cloud over the Poles rarely breaching 25,000ft while giant thunder clouds in the tropics can stretch up to 60-70,000ft. On the North Atlantic cloud build up rarely creates problems for overflying aircraft as vertical thunder cloud limits in the region seldom reach the normal cruise levels of around 31-37,000ft. The large number of aircraft on the North Atlantic route systems are required to adhere precisely to track so any lack of heavy cloud at altitude is perhaps just as well. Lateral separation between tracks is 60nm and longitudinal separation between aircraft on the same track is 15 minutes. Vertical separation on the same track is 2,000ft but aircraft on adjacent tracks may be at the same level. Jets at the same height, therefore, travelling in the same direction on different tracks have a lateral separation of

only 60nm, which is not a lot in a crowded sky. Normally deviating 30nm to avoid weather is considered a minor detour, but on the North Atlantic track system it would be deemed a major change of course. If two aircraft on adjacent tracks choose to avoid separate weather cells by turning towards each other, the potential conflict is obvious. Since deviation from track is seldom possible, aircraft have no choice but to ride out any adverse weather en route, although in remote area, or under radar, obtaining permission to detour large cumulus cloud is normally a simple matter. At all times a wary eye is kept for bad weather and when in cloud, weather radar is switched on to pinpoint turbulent cells. The radar scanner emits a pulse which is reflected from the large water droplets associated with cumulus cloud and displays the cloud formations as 'blobs' on the screen. Severe cloud build ups in the States, especially in summer, are not uncommon, and flights can generally avoid the worst using weather radar while under surveillance from ground-based radar control.

The time is now approaching 1700 and the First Officer tunes in New York met broadcasts on 6,604KHz using HF2. Forecast and actual weather is transmitted continuously on four different HF frequencies from New York for major eastern states destinations. Airports in a particular area are grouped together in blocks of about half a dozen and the information transmitted over a five-minute period. Detroit and Chicago forecasts are broadcast hourly from on the hour to five past, New York, Boston and Washington from 10 to 15 past, and Montreal and Toronto (broadcast from Gander on the

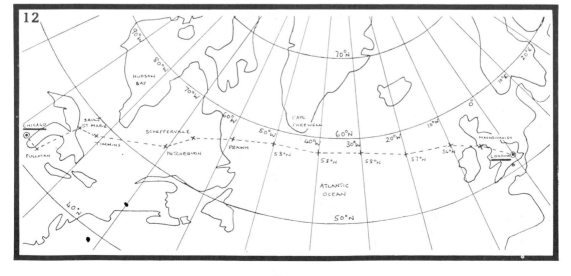

same frequencies) from 20 to 25 past. The Co-pilot copies the Chicago and Detroit weather and passes the details to the Captain who notes with pleasure that the expected weather has not materialised and that the forecast is much improved. For the time of arrival in Chicago the prognosis is sky clear, visibility 6nm with a wind of 040° at 15kt. A nice day!

An alert light on the INS now glows orange indicating the approach of 30°W and the way points are once again checked for accuracy. As the jet banks on to the new course, times and estimates are noted and the Co-pilot attempts contact with Gander on HF1 on frequency 5,649KHz. Meanwhile the Captain prepares to copy the weather for New York, Boston and Washington due at 10 past on HF2. After several attempts contact is not established with Gander and the secondary frequency of 8,879KHz is selected.

First Officer R/T 'Gander Speedbird two nine eight on eight eight seven nine, position.'
Gander R/T 'Speedbird two nine eight, go ahead.'
First Officer R/T 'Roger, Gander, negative contact on five six four nine. Copy Shanwick, please. We checked five eight north three zero west at one seven zero six, level three five zero, estimating five eight north four zero west at one seven four five, five eight north five zero west next. Temperature is minus six one, wind zero five zero at two zero.'

Gander repeats, and the message is confirmed correct by the First Officer. Speedbird 298 is now past the position considered the halfway crossing point for flights to east coast destinations, but for the route to Chicago flight time remaining is still about 5½hr. 'November juliet' has been airborne for 2½hr with about 2hr remaining to complete the ocean crossing leaving approximately 3½hr to fly the 1,400nm across Canada and the States from the coast of Labrador to Chicago.

Speedbird 298 is speeding westwards against the spinning earth and manages to keep up a little with the setting sun. Its speed however, is no match for the peripheral velocity of the globe and the sun begins to lower itself in the sky, albeit more slowly than normal. The glowing sun now pierces the flightdeck windows and glare shields are fitted in place by the pilots to relieve the brightness. At this stage the aircraft experiences some clear air turbulence (CAT) caused by light wind shear, and bumps around a little in the sky. It is a while since the crew have eaten and by this stage they are feeling hungry, so the turbulence instantly indicates that it must be meal time. Although it's only joked that turbulence usually commences when meals are about to be served (any unsteadiness being directly related to the temperature of the food; ie very hot soup equals severe turbulence) it is uncanny how often it happens! In the cabin the passengers have now finished their meals and the duty free service is complete. The cabin staff arrange screens to show the movies, with a different film being shown in each cabin area. Now with some time to spare Stewardess Sue Latham prepares the crew meal and asks

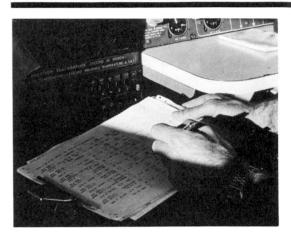

Above:
The Flight Engineer completes his first fuel check.

Below:
Approaching 30 West the INS way points are re-checked for the next leg of the flight.

each his choice of course. The selection, mind you, is not exactly limitless, as flight crew meals are prepared independently of the passengers, but the main courses are normally of good simple fare such as steak, lamb or chicken. Meals are eaten from trays on laps while sitting at the controls and the Co-pilot eats a different meal from the Captain and at a different time. The Flight Engineer, somehow, always seems to get left with the chicken, and it is now joked that liking it has become a qualification for the job!'

Dehydration on long flights is also a problem as the atmosphere in the cabin is drier than normal owing to the lack of moisture in the ambient air being drawn into the aircraft via compressors. (A bread roll can be seen to dry up quickly if left open on a tray.) Humidifiers are normally switched on in flight to add moisture to the cabin air but rarely produce normal conditions. Crews are advised to keep up their fluid intake by drinking tea, coffee or soft drinks approximately every 20min, and cabin crews are usually very helpful in popping into the flightdeck from time to time with the requested beverages. On one occasion when the cabin crew were busier than normal and had been unable to attend the flight crew for a while, one rather dry-throated Captain sent back a note which read, 'We surrender, please send water!'

The light chop (ie bumpy air) felt earlier now abates and smooth flight returns. At times on the North Atlantic run light to moderate turbulence is experienced caused by the strong westerly winds which are a normal feature of the area, and on occasions even severe turbulence is encountered. The strong winds are associated with the Polar front and are a product of the marked drop in temperature found at the borders between widely differing warm and cold air masses. The atmosphere cools with height at a rate of approximately 2°C per thousand feet, and this cooling continues until a point is reached at which the temperature is considered to remain constant at around −57°C. The lower levels at which this standard rate occurs is known as the troposphere. Where the temperature remains constant is known as the stratosphere and the dividing line between the two as the tropopause. At mid latitudes the average height of the tropopause varies from winter to summer from about 30,000 to 35,000ft. Clouds are the result of moisture within the atmosphere condensing when moist air is cooled on rising and the tropopause is important to pilots because it

generally marks the height limit of cloud formation, and also indicates the maximum height of strong winds. Over the North Atlantic, at the sharp division between warm and cold air masses, the steep gradient of the tropopause, and the resultant effects of temperature and pressure at height, compound to produce aloft winds of enormous speeds. Where the wind is concentrated into a fast flowing river of air of only a few miles deep, but perhaps a hundred or more miles wide and a thousand miles long, it is known as a jet stream, and speeds at its centre can reach 200kt. Wind speed from the core to the edges of the stream tapers off rapidly and results in a shear effect between the varying layers causing CAT. Attempts are made to forecast areas of CAT which are not always successful. Unfortunately there is no device at present on the flightdeck to detect such turbulence and it can often catch flights unawares and give them a bit of a shaking. Conversely, areas of forecast CAT are frequently quite smooth. Sitting with seat belts fastened at all times is the best precaution. The high wind velocities found at jet stream cores are generally avoided by westbound flights but are used by opposite direction traffic to 'push' the flight along. Eastbound aircraft can, on the rare occasion, experience ground speeds in excess of 700kt. The average wind component on the North Atlantic, however, is westerly at 60kt which normally adds up to one hour to a UK to US flight compared to an easterly crossing.

Speedbird 298 passes 120nm south of Cape Farewell on the southern tip of Greenland but cloud cover obscures most of the land from view. A voice from another flight comes over the speaker on 121.5MHz passing a message to Clipper 125 to call Gander on 8,879KHz. It is not strictly correct to use the emergency channel in this manner but often it's the only way to contact an aircraft who may be using a different frequency. Pan Am does not respond so he may be out of range or perhaps still attempting contact on HF. With 'november juliet' well within the Gander area the westbound squawk code of A3000 is now set in the transponder. All flights bound for Canada are expected to squawk this code as an aid to identification at least 30min before the Gander control boundary.

The Cabin Services Officer (CSO) now pops into the flightdeck to say that a number of passengers are asking about the final scores of the two big rugby internationals played that afternoon, so the First Officer tunes the BBC World Service on 5975KHz to listen to sports

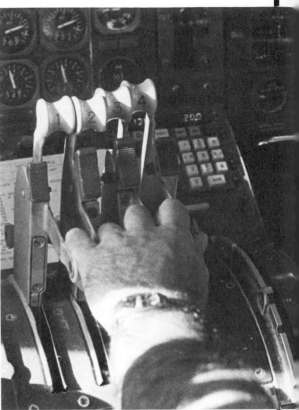

Above:
The North Atlantic track speed is 0.84 Mach, and as the Mach meter increases to 0.861 . . .

Right:
. . . the Flight Engineer reduces power to slow the aircraft. To the right of the thrust levers can be seen the keyboard of the INS.

Fig 13:
Significant Weather chart — North Atlantic.

round up at quarter to the hour. The movies are still showing in the cabin, so the Captain lets the CSO know that if he obtains the results he'll inform the passengers on his next PA announcement over Labrador. At position 40°W the time is 1745 GMT, and the navigation and communication procedures are once again repeated. The latest fuel check is also performed and the figures show a healthy situation with 19.9 tonnes remaining at destination which is one tonne up on estimated requirements. Meanwhile the Captain listens to the World Service and notes the rugby scores.

Of the Flight Crew's many checks throughout the year the most important are the bi-annual visits to the 'sweat box' known as the simulator. Such devices used to be jokingly referred to as 'cock ups of mock pits' but are now highly sophisticated pieces of equipment with movement in all directions, and very realistic visual displays. Within these 'flying' machines crews face a multitude of drills and emergencies during their refreshers and checks which would not be experienced in ten lifetimes of flying. Today aircraft are extremely reliable, and normally the only chance of practicing unusual circumstances is

in the simulator. During the four-hour sessions work load is very high and crews are constantly under pressure. Drills such as flap failures, abandoned take-offs, landing gear problems, and emergency procedures are frequently and thoroughly reviewed. The instrument rating test must also be taken (and passed) annually, and throughout the 'flight' test, speeds, heights, and headings must be flown within strict limits. The simulator is not referred to as the 'sweat box' for nothing.

Trans-oceanic flights face their own special problems in an emergency. Some incidents, such as cargo hold fires, for example, call for landing at the nearest suitable airport once drills have been completed. Since there aren't too many airports in the middle of the Atlantic a little reconsideration is required. A single engine failure case can also be exacerbated by circumstances. With such a vast stretch of ocean to cover the crew not only have to consider the present conditions but must also prepare for the unlikely event of another engine failing. Even the simple decision whether a flight should continue with one engine out, or turn back, has to be arrived at with caution. Gander in Canada, and Shannon in Eire are two useful onward or

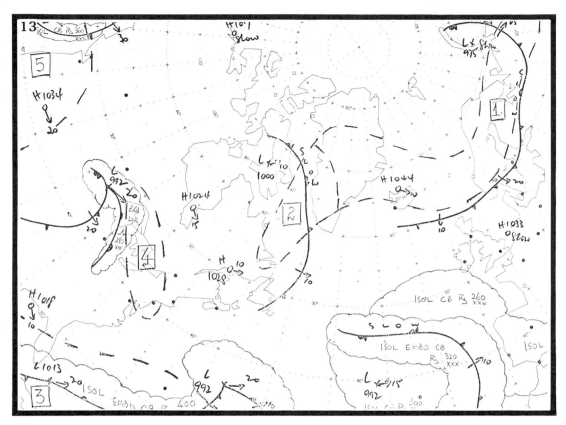

return alternates, that is provided the weather is satisfactory. If not, others have to be found. An equal time point between the two can then be calculated, which takes into account the prevailing wind, and aircraft position relative to the equal time point influences the course of action. The loss of one engine on a four-jet aircraft, however, does not normally pose a problem, except that, with the resultant loss of some power, the aircraft may have to descend into the more dense atmosphere to maintain cruise. At all times the Flight Engineer notes the three-engine cruise height required for actual aircraft weight. As fuel is consumed the three-engine cruise level increases with decreasing weight, and at light weights may be the same, or even above, the present four-engine cruise level, in which case the flight simply continues as before. It is at this point, however, that the Flight Engineer normally has his little joke and informs the Captain that 'in the event of an engine failure *climb* to the three-engine cruise height of level 360'.

Recent aviation controversy has centred on the proposed use of such twin-engined jets as the Boeing 757 and 767, and the Airbus, on the North Atlantic, the argument in favour being the reliability of modern engines. Failure rate, however, no matter how low, does not rule out the possibility of engine loss, and although the failure of one on a four-engined jet is inconvenient, engine failure on a twin jet over the ocean could be considered an emergency. Future developments will be interesting to view.

Loss of pressurisation is another incident compounded by the isolation of the great oceans. The siutation can be successfully contained by initiating an emergency descent. Oxygen masks are donned by the flight crew and passenger masks drop automatically from the cabin ceiling. The Captain closes the thrust levers, selects speed brake, lowers the landing gear at the appropriate speed, and disconnects the autopilot. The aircraft is then turned off track and the nose pushed sharply down until maximum speed is achieved. With so much drag the aircraft descends at an amazing 10,000ft plus per minute. Although an uncomfortable experience for the passengers the manoeuvre is perfectly safe. At 14,000ft the aircraft is levelled off and, once again, an instruction from the check list states 'land at the nearest suitable airport'. Now the problems begin. For a start the crew must remain on oxygen at 14,000ft, and must not remove masks until below 10,000ft, although the passengers at this height are permitted to breathe freely. An inspection of the arc of available land from the UK to Canada shows airports available in Scotland, Iceland, Greenland and Labrador, but with severe winter weather in the north many will be closed. Fuel consumption with a fully laden jumbo at such a low level is something just above astronomical, so range is limited. Sharp pencils and quick minds in a rather uncomfortable environment are the order of the day. Why not remain at altitude with everyone on oxygen? Two reasons: at height the rate of oxygen usage would be just above astronomical as well, thereby creating a similar problem, and it could also get cold. Aviation, anyway, works on the 'belt and braces' principle whereby an alternative must always be available. The naked sword hanging over the head of Damocles by a single

Left:
The Co-pilot copies the Chicago and Detroit weather and passes the details to the Captain.

Below left:
Now with some time to spare the Stewardess, Sue Latham, prepares the crew meal . . .

Bottom left:
. . . and asks each his choice of main course.

Fig 14:
Flight Log — Dean's Cross to Prawn.

Fig 15:
Radio Navigation chart — Gander OCA.

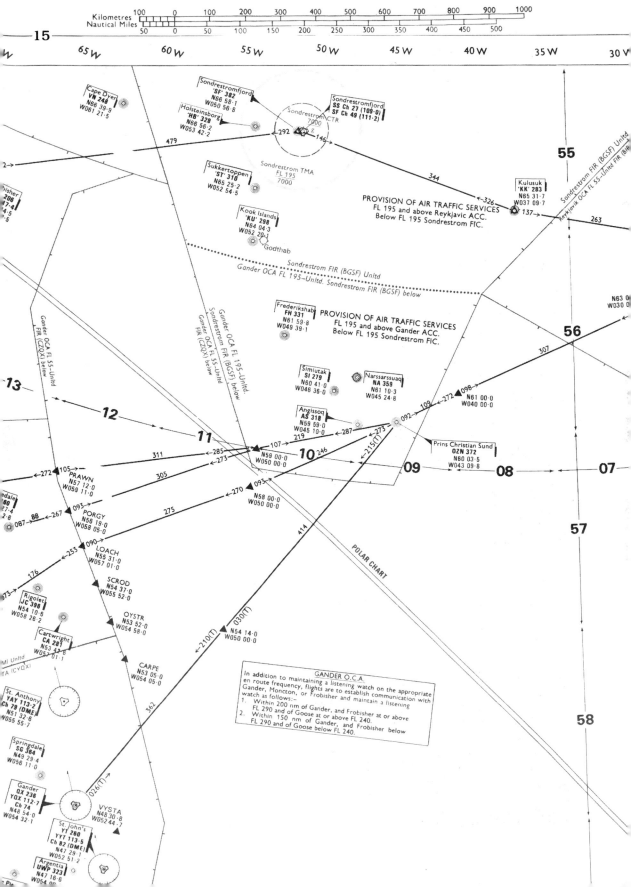

horse hair may have been a wonderful demonstration of the fragility of life, but not one that should be enacted too often. Flight crew exist in a much more practical world and are well aware that any exposure to a sharp pointed sword would almost certainly be the one time the horse hair *would* break. At 35,000ft a human being can remain conscious for about 90sec with an instantaneous loss of oxygen. Imagine an aircraft remaining aloft after a pressurisation failure with the passengers and crew on emergency oxygen. Any failure of the oxygen system would not permit sufficient time for descent. Such a situation is unacceptable. Incidentally, failure of the emergency oxygen in cruise creates the same problem. In spite of the fact that the pressurisation system may be working normally, the 'belt' of the 'belt and braces' is considered lost, and a descent must be initiated.

One rather obvious emergency in flights over oceans which requires consideration, no matter however remote the possibility, is ditching in the sea. Such a situation would almost certainly arise from an aircraft running out of fuel, and is a most unlikely event. The crew, however, must be prepared for every eventuality and ditching is no exception.

A life jacket is placed below each seat and its use demonstrated before the start of every overseas flight. On the Boeing 747, life rafts are stowed above the two over-wing exits, while the other four main doors on either side have combined slide/rafts contained within the door structure. Opening of the doors automatically deploys the slide/rafts which can then be detached from the door mounting to float free of the aircraft when the passengers are safely aboard.

Simulator checks and refresher training are only part of the requirement for crews to maintain flying licences current. Medicals, technical tests, safety procedures checks, route flying checks etc, all have to be passed. Also, the art of flying is not dissimilar to the playing of a musical instrument in that frequent practice is required. Indeed, by law, a flight crew member must fly once every 28 days, any relapse requiring a re-check before flying can be commenced. Standards amongst flight crews are, of necessity, high, but the required abilities are often humorously stated to be: Captain — must be able to read *and*

write; First Officer — must be able to read *or* write; Flight Engineer — must *know* someone who can read or write.

At 50°W the aircraft automatically turns for Prawn, a named position on the edge of Moncton control area, some 100nm from the Canadian coast. INS details are checked again and fresh way point positions inserted. Wind strength is more normal now, and the ground speed has dropped to 453kt.

First Officer R/T 'Gander, Speedbird two nine eight on eighty eight, position.'
Gander R/T 'Speedbird two nine eight, Gander, go ahead.'

Below left:
Meals are eaten from trays while sitting at the controls.

Below:
The Co-pilot eats a different meal from the Captain and at a different time.

Bottom:
The light chop felt earlier now abates and smooth flight returns.

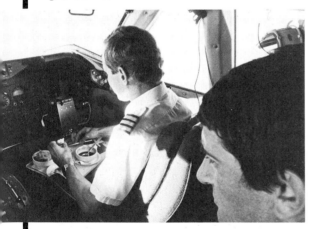

First Officer R/T 'Gander, Speedbird two nine eight checked five eight north five zero west at one eight two six, level three five zero, estimate Prawn at one nine zero six, Schefferville next. Temperature minus five six, wind two zero zero at six zero.'
Gander R/T 'Roger, Speedbird two nine eight, copied OK. At Prawn call Moncton on one two eight decimal seven.'

The pilots now prepare the North American charts and check out the high level and jet airways routeings to Chicago. Most Canadian and American aviation charts are printed by Jeppesen, a company started by Elrey Jeppesen, the son of a Danish cabinet maker who began flying in the 1920s in Portland, USA. Jepp's pioneering career began as an airmail pilot on the most difficult of routes. After the winter of 1930, when four pilots were killed on a particularly dangerous run, Jepp set about compiling details of routes in a little black book which soon became a source of interest to other pilots. Eventually demand became so great that Jeppesen went into the publishing business with his first *Airway Manual*, and the present company was born. Speedbird 298's routeing across North America is checked on charts against the flight plan, the details of which will already have been telexed to the Canadian authorities. An en route clearance, however, is still required, and will be issued at Prawn by Moncton control.

In the cabin the movies are just finishing and afternoon tea is to be served shortly. Ahead the sky is clear, but the atmosphere is hazy, and below the rough sea is only just discernible. A few large icebergs can be seen directly below the nose. Once again, with the change of wind, (and, of course, with the approach of tea) the aircraft begins to buffet, gently at first, but then more violently, in the choppy air. The Captain switches on the seat belt signs. Such moments are often the worst for passengers, being shaken in the close confines of the cabin. Invariably some feel a little nauseous, and many more, quite unnecessarily, feel apprehensive. Modern aircraft are built with incredible strength, and turbulence damage to aircraft in flight is extremely rare. To see a modern aircraft tested to destruction in a special rig, where the wings are bent upwards and only break when the points are near to touching, would dispel the fears of most! The bumpy conditions last for about 10min and then smooth flight returns. The Captain switches off the

seat belt signs and afternoon tea, with sandwiches and scones, commences.

On each sector over three hours the Flight Engineer is expected to complete an engine condition monitoring log with information on all engine parameters. The readings are, preferably, recorded within the first hour of cruise, although it is not always practicable, and at this quiet moment in the flight the opportunity is taken to document the details. The thrust levers are first adjusted to the required power setting on each before engine and flight readings are meticulously recorded. Thrust levers are connected by long cables to fuel control units which occasionally mis-set, resulting in lever misalignment, so lever positions are also noted against a scale on the pedestal. Any adjustment required is conducted at the next hangar check. Rarely in the cruise do thrust levers fall precisely in line so some stagger is to be expected. On occasions, however, misalignment can result in throttle stagger of a few inches between each, a condition known in the trade as a 'bunch of bananas'! Engine details noted on the monitoring log by the Flight Engineer are then compared with calculated performance data for present flight conditions and any trends noted. By such methods a performance devia-tion can be detected at an early stage and action taken.

Approaching the hour the First Officer pre-pares to copy the latest Chicago weather on HF2. Although earlier reports indicated a nice day, snow can move in quickly and it's as well to keep regular checks. The Boeing 747 can land on up to four inches of dry snow but on only up to half an inch of wet snow, so any falls could cause problems. Even with a light fall some runways would, no doubt, be closed for sweeping, and delays would be inevitable.

Above:
The Co-pilot now prepares the North American charts and checks out the high level and jet airways routeing to Chicago.

Above:
The 'sweat box' known as the simulator. The gantry surrounds the unit which produces the computer generated picture for visual display. The complete unit moves on hydraulic jacks seen at the bottom of the picture.

Left:
Inside the simulator is an exact working copy of the flight deck. The picture shows one of British Airways Boeing 747 simulators.

A heavy fall would probably close the airport, if only for a short period. When any major airport closes because of weather the ensuing upheaval is unbelievable. Controllers and flight crews have to play the situation by ear as aircraft scatter for open airports in all directions, with clearances being issued over the air. When the busiest airport in the world closes the situation can only be imagined. It is as well to be prepared! At such times, all aviation personnel, whether on the ground or in the air, earn their money by the sweat of their brows. Today, however, the latest Chicago report is, once again, a surprise. The present weather is showing partly cloudy, visibility seven statute miles, wind 045/15, with a temperature of 53°F — a relative heatwave! Although bitterly cold winters in the northern states are the norm, freak winds can bring warm dry weather for short periods. In the eastern Rockies, for example, the Chinook wind can change the temperature by 20°C or more, with conditions leaping from say -10°C to +10°C in a matter of hours.

At 1906 the aircraft turns over Prawn. Although outside the range of civil radar the flight's progress at this point is most definitely being observed by the military as Speedbird 298 approaches the Atlantic coastal Canadian identification zone. The outside temperature is showing -49°C and the wind 210/65.

First Officer R/T 'Moncton, Speedbird two nine eight heavy, good afternoon, just passed Prawn level three five zero.'

In North America, 'heavy' is added to call signs on initial contact with air traffic control to indicate a big jet.

No reply. Other aircraft ahead are heard in contact with the controller so 'november juliet' will shortly be in range. The Schefferville VOR beacon frequency of 112.7MHz is selected on both sets, but lying some 290nm away on the Labrador/Quebec border is still out of range. After 10min a second attempt establishes contact and the flight level and estimate of Shefferville of 1946 are passed

Moncton R/T 'Roger, Speedbird two nine eight, you're cleared to Chicago via North American route three two four. Maintain level three five zero.'

The First Officer repeats the clearance

Captain 'Ask him for three seven zero, please.'

Normal westbound flight levels are 310, 350 and 390. Speedbird 298 is too heavy for 390, but often requests for opposite direction levels are granted in North America if traffic permits.

First Officer R/T 'Moncton, Speedbird two nine eight, requesting level three seven zero.'
Moncton R/T 'Roger, two nine eight, standby.'

Direct routeings are also frequently requested as aircraft make landfall over the coast of Canada, but today Speedbird 298's routeing is satisfactory. A favourite request for flights with eastern seaboard destinations is from the Canadian coast right down to the town of Kennebunk, some 700nm away. Kennebunk lies near the coast of Maine about 65nm north of Boston. It may not be internationally recognised like New York or Philadelphia, but the town is world famous to all trans-Atlantic flight crew, although few will ever have been there. The Captain checks route 324 from the Western supplement from Schefferville on airways high level and jet 548 to Pullman, then victor 84 to Pappi, and on to Chicago, and confirms these details against the flight plan routeing. In Canada upper airways above 18,000ft are designated as high level airways and in the States as jet routes. Below, all airways are named victor.

North American routeings have been in use for some time now whereby a single number defines a complete route, but before their introduction full airways clearances had to be issued in detail. For some reason the routeing from the Canadian coast to Washington DC always turned out to be the most complicated — high level 579 to Stephenville, high level 581 to Fredericton, jet and high level 581 to Bangor, jet 49 to Albany, jet 75 to . . . It needed a quick hand and alert mind to copy the clearance rapidly and accurately before read back. One crew felt it was time to play the controllers at their own game and decided to request the routeing as filed rather than wait for the clearance. On first contact with the Canadian controller the position report was passed, followed immediately by . . .' and requesting high level 579 to Stephenville, high level 581 to Fredericton, jet and high level 581 to Bangor, jet 49 to . . .' and so on. There was a rather pregnant pause before the controller replied, somewhat sheepishly, 'can you say again please'. Touché! North American route numbers are much simpler.

Moncton R/T 'Speedbird two nine eight, Moncton.'
First Officer R/T 'Speedbird two nine eight, go ahead.'
Moncton R/T 'Speedbird two nine eight, unable higher, Air Canada flight ahead of you at three seven zero bound for Montreal on your routeing. Squawk two six three zero.'
First Officer R/T 'Ah yes, we've been following Air Canada across the 'pond' and we wondered about his routeing. OK, we'll maintain three five zero. Squawking now two six three zero.'
Moncton R/T 'Thank you two nine eight, you're radar identified. Omit position reports.'

The high ground of Labrador can now be seen ahead through the haze. Below ice floes and packed ice are seen clearly on the crazed surface of the frozen sea, but the coastline is mostly indiscernible on the snow-bound landscape. The VOR beacon at Schefferville comes within range and the orange beam bar of the compass system lies central indicating INS tracking is good. The Captain picks up the hand set to speak to the passengers.

Captain PA 'Good afternoon ladies and gentlemen, the Captain speaking once again from the flightdeck. We're now over Labrador

Above:
The Captain switches off the seat belt signs and afternoon tea . . .

Below:
. . . with sandwiches and scones, commences.

in Canada, level at thirty five thousand feet. Flight time remaining is just over three hours and we're still estimating arrival in Chicago on schedule at quarter to five. The route from here takes us to Schefferville on the Labrador/Quebec border, then we head south west bound right down across Quebec. We pass into Ontario about 120 miles south of Hudson Bay and from there we proceed to Sault St Marie on the Canadian/US border, at the confluence of three of the great lakes. We then pass down the east coast of Lake Michigan before turning westbound for Chicago. The flight from now should be smooth, and the Chicago weather is fine. The latest temperature we have at one o'clock Chicago time is fifty three degrees Fahrenheit, that's eleven centigrade. For the rugby fans on board I can give you the final scores. Wales beat Scotland 19-15, and Ireland beat France, 22-16.'

In the cabin afternoon tea service is just finishing and the last of the trays are being removed. 'November juliet' has been airborne for about five hours now, and with lunch, movie and afternoon tea complete, a number of passengers are beginning to get a little restless. Some are moving about the aisles stretching their legs. A few are asking if they can visit the flightdeck and the CSO asks the Captain for permission. Policy on flightdeck visits varies from airline to airline and from country to country. On US aircraft, for example, passengers are not permitted by FAA regulations to visit the flight deck at any time in flight. The main objection voiced, of course, is the risk of hijack, although it's generally accepted that a determined terrorist armed with a modern weapon could easily overpower an unarmed crew by force. Some airlines carry armed sky marshalls, but the thought of a shoot out in mid-flight is an uncomfortable prospect for most crews. Past experience has shown that hijacking rarely, if ever, results in an aircraft accident, and that the line of least resistance is normally the best approach for everyone. An acknowledgement of the hijacker's authority (Question — what do you call a terrorist with a gun at your head? Answer — Sir!), and compliance with demands, but without total submssion, is usually the safest approach.

Those who most enjoy a visit to the flight-deck are the children. A test switch on the pilot's overhead panel, and a similar control by the Flight Engineer, can be activated to illuminate simultaneously all the emergency lights on the flight deck. At night the Christmas tree effect is spectacular, and the sight of wonder on the visitors' little faces as they gasp at the scene is a joy to behold.

Most passengers invited to view comment on the small size of the flightdeck, especially on the Boeing 747, but with the requirement to have levers and switches within reach of all crew members it's necessary to position the seats and panels close together. It is also a little noisier than the cabin with a light rush of air being heard in the background. The apparent lack of movement with clouds far below seemingly quite stationary is also frequently remarked upon. Children often ask why the plane has stopped!

Speedbird 298 banks over Schefferville as the VOR needles turn and point rearwards. The NDB beacon at Nitchequon in northern Quebec, frequency 364KHz, is tuned on both automatic direction finders. Although 176nm away the beacon power is strong and the needles indicate direction.

Moncton R/T 'Speedbird two nine eight, Montreal now, one three three decimal five.'

The First Officer changes frequency.

First Officer R/T 'Montreal, Speedbird two nine eight heavy, good afternoon, we're level three five zero.'

Montreal R/T 'Thank you two nine eight. Maintain three five zero. Radar identified, omit position reports.'

'November juliet's' position is well out of range of normal VHF coverage from Montreal control, but relay stations along route retransmit the signals to the main centre. Being so far north there are few aircraft in the area, and since position reports are not required with positive radar identification, the radio is very quiet. Northern Canada is a remote and sparsely populated area, and even the chart states in bold letters that the land is unsurveyed. In the far northwest altimeter pressure settings are unavailable and aircraft fly on standard pressure settings at all times.

Speedbird 298 is being navigated by the INS with reference to true north. The compass can also be switched to true north alignment, but while on airways is selected to indicate magnetic direction. Magnetic north lies on the Canadian island of Bathurst some 1,000nm from true north, and variation, the angular different between true and magnetic north, is marked on charts. At such latitudes in the proximity of magnetic north rapid changes of variation result. At the Canadian coast variation is shown as 32°W, and at Chicago, zero. For light aircraft navigating from charts in the region the correct application of variation is of prime importance.

As the beacon at Nitchequon slips beneath the nose Speedbird 298 adjusts heading to track the centre line of airway high level 548 to the town of Timmins, in eastern Ontario, some one hour's flying away.

Montreal R/T 'Speedbird two nine eight, Air Canada has now turned south for Montreal on high level 545. Flight level three seven zero will be available in 15 minutes.'

The flight time remaining is now about two hours and is insufficient for cruise at 370 to save the fuel used in climbing higher.

First Officer R/T 'Speedbird two nine eight. We're happy at flight level three five zero.'

Montreal R/T 'OK Speedbird two nine eight. Maintain three five zero. In 10 minutes monitor me on one three four decimal nine.'

At the appropriate time Montreal centre is recontacted. Although a frequency change has been allocated, Speedbird 298 is still talking to the same controller through another relay station.

Montreal R/T 'Thank you, Speedbird two nine eight. Monitor me on this frequency all the way until 100 DME from Timmins, then contact Toronto on one three three decimal nine seven.'

Air traffic control in Canada is a mixture of American and English, but with the more formal approach of the British. In America it's quite different with foreign crews having to adapt their own speech to be understood. Whoever stated that America and Britain are two nations divided by a common language could not have put it more succinctly. A frequency of one three three decimal nine seven becomes one thirty three point ninety seven. Level three five zero becomes level three five oh. Speedbird two nine eight becomes Speedbird two ninety eight. On the ground and in the air an endless variety of English words have their American counterparts. Pavement becomes sidewalk; lift, elevator; braces, suspenders; and flat, apartment, etc.

Some word differences are almost deliberately designed to sow the maximum confusion. 'Fag' in the UK may be colloquial for a cigarette but in the States is slang for a

'gay' guy. To have a large hairy flight crew member say loudly in a New York bar that he's dying for a fag attracts more than a few curious glances!

British crews flying American built aircraft use American phraseology and end up with a mid-Atlantic vocabulary. Throttle becomes thrust lever; undercarriage, gear; HP cocks, start levers; variable tail plane, stabiliser. In the States 'overshoot' means to go off the end of the runway, while in the UK it means discontinue an approach and go-around again. Not surprisingly the Americans refer to such a manoeuvre simply as a 'go-around'. For tower control at Heathrow to instruct a US airline about to land to overshoot invariably invokes an expletive, or at best a surprised exclamation.

Not only is American langauge and spelling strange to the British, but dates are also written differently, with the month being placed first. 1.4.85 is not 1 April, but is 4 January, as, no doubt, many a European export agent has found to his cost. In department stores the ground floor is marked as the first floor. To go up two flights of stairs hoping to arrive at the second and find oneself on the

Above:
Once on each sector over three hours the Flight Engineer is expected to complete an engine condition monitoring log.

Right:
The engine instruments on the pilot's central panel. Engine instruments in line from top to bottom for each engine — engine pressure ratio, N1 (or fan) speed, exhaust gas temperature, fuel flow (in thousands of kilogrammes per hour — about 2,700kg per engine). Note instrument pointers lying in banks — any one out of line shows clearly. Bottom left is the pilot's warning lights panel, top left the standby horizon. Flap position indicators are seen to the right of the engine instruments, with the landing gear lever protruding far right.

third is most confusing. Light switches, too, operate differently than in England, up being 'on' and down 'off', which, incidentally is the same for switches on all aircraft, American or otherwise. Apparently the accidental flicking down of a switch is more likely, and it's deemed safer to have equipment switched off by such an involuntary movement than on. Other differences on the flightdeck are the use of aviation units. America still operates to a modified imperial system with height in feet, speed in knots, distance in nautical miles, runway length in feet, weight in pounds, temperature in degrees Fahrenheit, pressure in inches of mercury, landing visibility in feet and statute miles, and volume in US gallons. The UK operates to the International Civil Aviation Organisation (ICAO) standards, which have been adopted by most of the world except, notably, the Soviet Union, China and, of course, the States, with height in feet, speed in knots, distance in nautical miles, runway length in metres, weight in kilogrammes, temperature in degrees centigrade, pressure in millibars, landing visibility in metres and kilometres, and volume in litres. When operating within the

States aircraft which comply with ICAO standards have to convert just about every unit for calculations on the ground before departure.

At 100nm on the distance measuring equipment from Timmins the Co-pilot flicks the No 1 VHF switch to select the dialled Toronto frequency of 133.97MHz.

First Officer R/T 'Toronto, Speedbird two nine eight heavy, good afternoon, we're level three five zero.'
Toronto R/T 'Speedbird two nine eight, good afternoon, maintain three five zero. Confirm squawking two three six zero.'
First Officer R/T 'Speedbird two nine eight, that's affirmative.'
Toronto R/T 'Roger, Speedbird two nine eight, you're radar identified 95 miles northeast of Timmins. Call me at Timmins on this frequency, please.'
First Officer R/T 'OK, call you Timmins.'

'November juliet' is now over Ontario with the southern tip of Hudson Bay lying 120nm to the north. The ground below is blanketed in snow and in the hazy conditions visibility is

poor. Ahead can be seen the tops of some large cumulus cloud protruding above the horizon, and the weather radar is switched on to check range and intensity. One large 'blob' on the radar screen lies on the range marker centre line indicating a big thunder cloud sitting directly on track. The wind is blowing from the northwest at 60kt so any turbulent air will lie to the southeast in the wake of the thunder cell.

Captain 'When we get a bit nearer you'd better ask if we can deviate to the north.'

After five minutes the large cloud looms closer and it's decided that about a 15nm detour is required.

First Officer R/T 'Toronto, Speedbird two nine eight. We'd like to deviate to the north about 15 miles to avoid build up.'
Toronto R/T 'OK, Speedbird two nine eight, that's approved. Call me back on track.'

The Captain disengages the inertial navigation system and selects heading mode on the autopilot switching. By gentle movement of the button-sized heading control knob the giant jumbo jet is turned 30° to the right. A line of cloud is seen stretching further than

expected but does not indicate on radar the presence of any turbulent cloud other than the cell on track. Shortly Speedbird 298 enters the cloudy atmosphere, but flight remains smooth with the aircraft lying to windward of the thunder area. Engine anti-icing is switched on and hot air is tapped from engine compressors to spray engine nacelles

Above:
The Co-pilot reads the thrust lever positions noted against a scale on the pedestal.

Below:
At 19.06 the aircraft turns over Prawn.

to maintain the intakes free of ice. Engine instrument probes are also kept free of ice to prevent erratic power indications. Ice build up in flight can be be very dangerous and every effort is made to avoid its occurrence. One example of ice accretion is rime ice which forms as a result of supercooled water droplets freezing on contact with the aircraft. These droplets actually maintain their liquid state in the atmosphere at temperatures below freezing point. On impact the droplets spread and freeze. Where there is little spreading, air becomes trapped between the particles producing an opaque appearance, but where spreading occurs clear translucent ice results. Any ice build up on engine leading edges can cause serious problems. Not only can airflow through the engines be disturbed but large chunks of ice falling free into the intake can result in extensive engine damage. Not surprisingly engine anti-icing is used frequently as a precautionary measure. Icing on aircraft leading edges of wings is a rare occurrence although airframe anti-icing is available if required. Any build up of ice on window posts indicates the presence of airframe icing and, once again, hot air can be tapped from engine compressors to supply wing leading edges.

Speedbird 298 breaks free of cloud and engine anti-icing is switched off. With the cloud cell well to the south 'november juliet' is turned for Timmins.

Captain 'Ask him for direct Sault St Marie, please.'
First Officer R/T 'Toronto, Speedbird two nine eight. We're in the clear now, request direct Sault St Marie.'
Toronto R/T 'OK Speedbird two nine eight, you're cleared direct Sault St Marie. Abeam Timmins call Toronto on one three two decimal six five.'

The Sault St Marie VOR co-ordinates are already inserted in way point 8 and the Captain keys 0-8 on the INS to display track. The aircraft is then turned using the heading control knob to establish direct track and the INS re-engaged. Speedbird 298 is now on a direct routeing for Sault St Marie. The beacon frequency of 112.2MHz is selected on both and the distance measuring equipment shows the VOR to be 180nm away.

Passing abeam Timmins at 1213 GMT the Flight Engineer completes his final fuel check. With fine weather at both Chicago and Detroit the Captain nominates Detroit as the fuel diversion for final calculations, and the figures show about 20tonnes fuel remaining at destination. Approximately 12tonnes are required in case of diversion to Detroit leaving just over 8tonnes remaining for delays. Holding fuel consumption is calculated at the rate of 9tonnes/hr, so approximately 50min of waiting time is available if traffic is heavy. The First Officer changes frequency.

First Officer R/T 'Toronto, Speedbird two nine eight heavy, just passed abeam Timmins level three five zero.'

No reply. A second attempt has the same negative result. Switching back to the original frequency control is informed.

Toronto R/T 'OK, Speedbird, two nine eight, try Toronto frequency one three three one five.'

The Co-pilot makes the necessary selection.

First Officer R/T 'Toronto, Speedbird two nine eight, do you read.'
Toronto R/T 'Loud and clear, Speedbird two nine eight. Maintain level three five zero and confirm squawking two three six oh.'
First Officer R/T 'That's affirmative, and maintaining level three five zero.'
Toronto R/T 'Roger, Speedbird two nine eight, call Toronto now on one three four four two.'

Another selection

First Officer R/T 'Toronto, Speedbird two nine eight, level three five zero. Proceeding direct Sault St Marie.'
Tortonto R/T 'Thank you, Speedbird two nine eight. Remain this frequency.'

Ahead the snow-frozen ground blends with the hazy atmosphere and visibility is still poor, although beginning to improve. Some small cumulus cloud can be seen dotting the horizon but nothing of significance is noted so the weather radar is switched off. Large cloud build up, in fact, is rare in winter and, surprisingly, icing conditions in flight are more of a problem in summer. In the warm, moist atmosphere, giant dark thunderclouds can form which are a distinct hazard to aviation. In Canada and the northern States weather in winter is more of a problem on the ground. Ice and snow lying on wings and fuselage surfaces is not permitted and de-icing is required. Hot de-icing fluid is hosed on all sur-

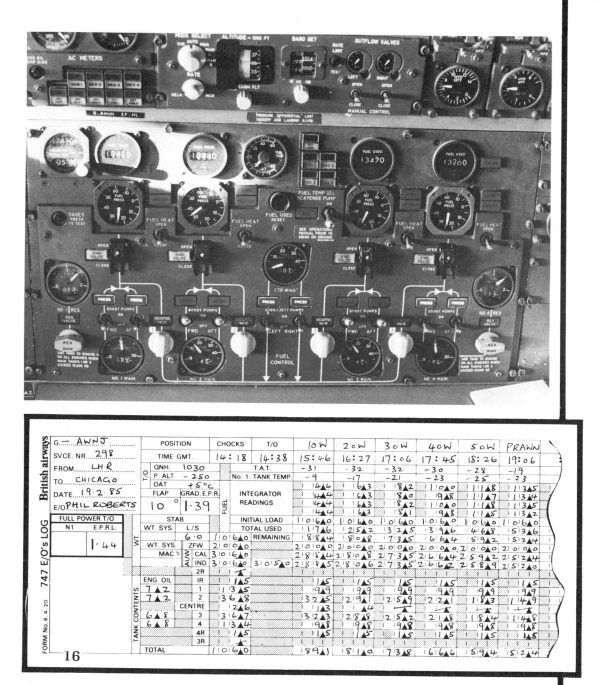

British airways

G - AWNJ
SVCE. NR. 298
FROM LHR
TO CHICAGO
DATE 19.2.85
E/O PHIL ROBERTS

FULL POWER T/O — N1 — E.P.R.L. — 1.44

747 E/O's LOG
FORM No. 8.4.2G

16

		CHOCKS	T/O	10W	20W	30W	40W	50W	PRAWN
POSITION									
TIME GMT.		14:18	14:38	15:46	16:27	17:06	17:45	18:26	19:06
QNH 1030	T.A.T.			-31	-32	-32	-30	-28	-19
P. ALT. -250	No. 1. TANK TEMP.			-9	-17	-21	-23	-25	-23
OAT +5°C	INTEGRATOR READINGS			1444	1643	1842	1040	1148	1345
FLAP 10° GRAD.E.P.R 1.39				1444	1643	1840	1948	1147	1344
				1444	1643	1842	1040	1148	1345
				1444	1643	1841	1948		
	INITIAL LOAD			101640	101640	101640	101640	101640	101640
STAB	TOTAL USED			11746	12542	31245	13946	14648	15346
WT. SYS. L/S 6.0	101640 REMAINING			81844	81048	17345	16644	15942	15244
WT. SYS. ZFW 20040		201040		201040	201040	201040	201040	201040	201040
MAC % CAL 30040				281842	281048	273345	261842	259242	252244
AUW IND 30160		30150		281845	280846	273345	261842	258349	252240
	2R								
ENG. OIL / IR			145	145	145	145	145	145	145
7 2	1	1345		1345	1949	1949	1949	949	949
7 2	2	3648		3245	2941	2549	2241	1843	1449
	CENTRE	1246		1143	144				
6 8	3	3647		3243	2848	2542	2148	1844	1148
6 8	4	1948		1948	1948	1948	1948	1948	1948
	4R	145		145	145	145	145	145	145
	3R								
	TOTAL	101640		18941	18110	17348	16646	15944	15244

faces to remove ice before departure. Any motorist knows the difficulty of driving on snow and ice, and taxying a machine of over 300 tonnes with 18 wheels in such conditions is no easy task. Turns are restricted to a maximum of 5kt. While taxying, snow banks at the edge of runways are also a hazard to the low slung outer engine pods, and slush and snow can be thrown up and can freeze on wheels, brakes and flaps causing problems.

Top:
The fuel panel showing fuel condition at Prawn. Note figures against the fuel monitoring log.

Fig 16:
Fuel Monitoring Log.

Right:
Packed ice and ice floes can be seen clearly — crossing the coast of Labrador in Newfoundland, Canada.

Ice and hard-packed snow on runways is a further hazard and wind gusts can compound the slippery surface conditions. Caution is the order of the day.

It is now just over one hour to arrival in Chicago and the crew are examining the aerodrome booklet. Chicago airport, in fact, was built during the war by Douglas Aircraft Corporation for the production of military transports, and was originally known as Orchard Place. It first opened to commercial traffic in 1955. In 1958, when international jet flights began to expand, the airport was renamed Chicago, O'Hare, after Lt Cdr Edward O'Hare, a World War 2 US Navy fighter pilot ace. On 20 February 1942, Lt Cdr O'Hare single handedly engaged an enemy formation of nine bombers intent on destroying his aircraft carrier. In repeated attacks five enemy aircraft were shot down and a sixth severely damaged before the formation reached its target. As a result the carrier escaped serious damage. His action was rewarded by a citation for bravery from President Roosevelt. Lt Cdr O'Hare was listed missing in action on 27 November 1944.

Since the war, airport expansion has continued in line with the increase in traffic and today there are no less than seven runways. At first sight Chicago's runway chart resembles the game of 'sticks', where a number are dropped at random and each has to be coaxed from the pile without moving the others. The runways are, of course, planned to cope with all prevailing wind directions and demonstrate quite clearly the variable conditions of the 'windy city'.

The last weather copied at 2100 GMT showed some scattered cloud at 9,000ft, visibility nine statute miles, temperature still 53°F, and a wind of 040/15, so both the easterly and northeasterly runways are probably in use. In the Chicago airport charts the appropriate runway plates are examined and landing details studied. Information such as safety heights, approach and missed approach procedures, instrument landing system (ILS) frequency and inbound track, outer marker position and height to cross above the marker on finals (as a check of the ILS glide path), runway threshold displaced or normal, approach and glide path lighting, and runway length etc, are noted. Runway lengths for 09L and 09R are 7,400 and 10,000ft respectively, and for 04L and 04R 7,500 and 8,000ft respectively, so both the

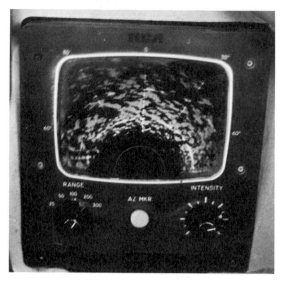

Above:

The weather radar is switched on to check range and intensity. 200nm range is selected, but the screen shows mostly ground returns. These can be eliminated by raising the scanner tilt.

Fig 17:
Radio Navigation chart — Northern Canada.

left runways are on the short side for the Boeing 747 with a minimum landing distance of 7,000ft. Approaching from the northeast the flight path to 09R is the shortest distance and, being the runway with the greatest length, is preferred for landing. However, with a fresh wind blowing the cross wind will be quite strong. On the shorter 04R runway, landing into wind will be more comfortable, but will probably not be possible owing to traffic sequencing.

The air traffic control clearance limit is Pappi, a position out over the lake at 16DME on the 077° radial from Northbrook VOR. Further clearance from Chicago radar is required to proceed beyond here. Any delays are absorbed at or before Pappi on one of the published holding patterns. Where a pattern is not shown all circling is to the right of a position. Aircraft, however, do not just arbitrarily go round in circles but precise holding patterns are flown with entry into the hold by correct procedure. These holds are the so-called 'stacks', where aircraft are piled one above the other at 1,000ft intervals. As flights from the bottom of the stack are cleared for approach those above move down in 1,000ft steps in turn.

In the latter stages of the cruise, at some

time before descent is commenced, it's required to 'guestimate' descent point from available information. Position Pappi lies on the extended centre line of O4L about 20nm from O'Hare. If an approach to 09R is allocated 'november juliet' will probably be required to cross Pappi at about 10,000ft.

Since cruise is at 35,000ft, a 25,000ft descent can be anticipated.

The distance out from a point to commence descent is extracted from a table showing distance required against height loss and speed, and adjusted for wind and aircraft weight. Speedbird 298's descent point is calculated to be 70nm from Pappi. The VOR at Pullman at the end of jet 548 on the east side of Lake Michigan is 67nm away from Pappi so descent can be commenced just before Pullman. In the US, however, ATC is notorious for pulling aircraft down early because of the intensity of traffic. It is doubtful if the calculated descent profile will be followed, but it's as well to be prepared.

Ahead from the flight deck can be seen the shore line of the Lakes and the icy surface as the visibility continues to improve.

Toronto R/T 'Speedbird two nine eight, Minneapolis now, one three three decimal eight five.'
First Officer R/T 'Speedbird two nine eight, good day.'

133.85MHz is selected.

First Officer R/T 'Minneapolis, good afternoon, Speedbird two ninety eight heavy level three five oh.'
Minneapolis R/T 'Level three five oh, Speedbird two ninety eight, good afternoon.'

The change of pace now is quite marked and already the flow of radio messages is increasing. The giant airports of Chicago and Detroit both lie to the south just 200nm apart and air traffic in the area is considerable. Over Sault St Marie at 2136 GMT Speedbird 298 banks left to track jet 548 to Traverse City, en route to Pullman some 30min flight time ahead. The Captain speaks to the passengers.

Captain PA 'Ladies and Gentlemen, Captain Murray speaking once again from the flight-deck. We've just passed over the town of Sault St Marie on the Canadian/US border and we're now in American airspace. Ahead lies Lake Michigan and on the left you can just seen the outline of Lake Huron through the cloud and on the right Lake Superior. Estimat-

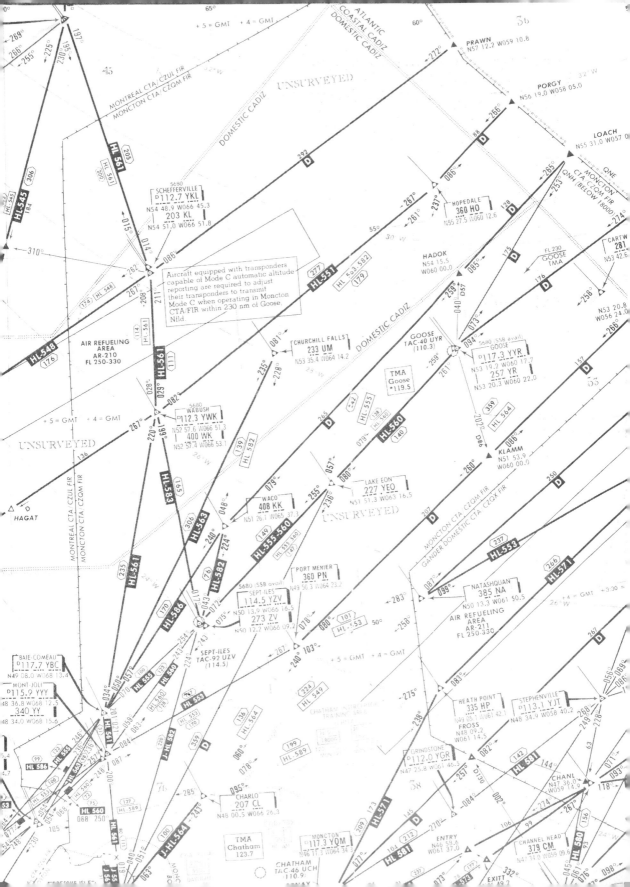

ing landing now in 50 minutes so arrival at the gate will be on schedule at a quarter to five, or perhaps even a few minutes earlier.'

Arinc frequency 129.4MHz is now dialled on VHF3 with selcal selected. Arinc is a US commercial communications organisation who pass urgent company messages as requested. Crews are alerted via selcal and any company information noted. If required the flightdeck can also be patched into the ground telephone network. The Chicago automatic terminal information service (ATIS) frequency of 135.15MHz is also selected on VHF2, but the aircraft is still lying out of range. It can be assumed from the forecast wind, however, that the 09R and 04R runways are in use, probably 09R for Speedbird 298 and the checks commenced accordingly. Any changes can be updated at a later stage.

In case of early descent the Captain now calls for the 'before descent check', which is once again read by the Flight Engineer with the two pilots responding to calls. The landing weight is estimated at 220 tonnes, and using this weight a minimum speed for crossing the runway threshold with full flap set (known as the reference speed, or V ref) is extracted from a table against aircraft weight. The indicated V ref speed of 130kt is noted on a landing data card together with minimum speeds for flap settings. The engine power required in the event of a go-around is also calculated for the present conditions and is noted as 1.41EPR. Other information noted includes details on landing limits, which are the minimum cloud base height and visibility acceptable for landing. With good weather forecast the Captain elects to fly a manual approach, so the hand held ILS limits of 970ft (above sea level) cloud break height, and 4,000ft visibility, are marked on the card. The height of the touchdown point for runway 09R is 670ft above sea level allowing a minimum cloud base height above the ground of 300ft.

All the speeds shown are bugged on the airspeed indicator (ASI) with 80kts, the speed at which reverse thrust is normally slowly reduced. 970ft is also marked on the pressure altimeters. On the Boeing 747, touch down heights are read from the radio altimeter with the pressure altimeter always reading height above sea level. On the ground at Chicago, therefore, the pressure altimeter will indicate the airport elevation of 670ft.

Continuing the before descent check the Flight Engineer sets the pressurisation for landing, humidifiers are switched off, instrument switching checked, seats and safety harnesses are checked locked and secure, landing data and limits are checked and set, and safety heights are noted. The Captain briefs the crew on the approach procedures, and ILS and beacon selection, outer marker height, landing limits, and action in the event of a go-around are all discussed. The safety height is also confirmed as 3,400ft. The land around O'Hare is, in fact, quite flat, but the tall skyscrapers of the city lying to the south east of the airport result in the safety height being high. The Flight Engineer announces the before descent check complete.

Minneapolis R/T 'Speedbird two ninety eight, Cleveland now, one thirty five sixty five.'

The First Officer dials 135,65MHz.

First Officer R/T 'Cleveland, Speedbird two ninety eight heavy level three five oh.'
Cleveland R/T 'Speedbird two ninety eight heavy, descend to two four oh.' Cleared direct Pappi.

Descent clearance, as suspected, has been given about 15min early.

First Officer R/T 'Speedbird two ninety eight, is that pilot discretion.'
Cleveland R/T 'Speedbird two ninety eight heavy, descend to cross sixty five miles northeast of Pappi level two four oh.'
First Officer R/T 'OK Speedbird two ninety eight, cleared direct Pappi to cross sixty five miles north east level two four oh. We'll call leaving three five oh.'

As 'november juliet' approaches Traverse City the Captain keys the INS to fly direct to Pappi 160nm to the south. Thirty nautical miles is required for the 11,000ft height loss down to level 240, so descent can be commenced in about 7min at 95nm out from Pappi.

At 2158 GMT the Captain initiates descent. 24,000ft is set in the altitude select window and the vertical speed wheel is wound down to 2,000ft/min. As the altimeter indicates Speedbird 298 leaving level 350 the Captain calls for descent power and the Flight

Fig 18:
Chicago O'Hare runway layout.

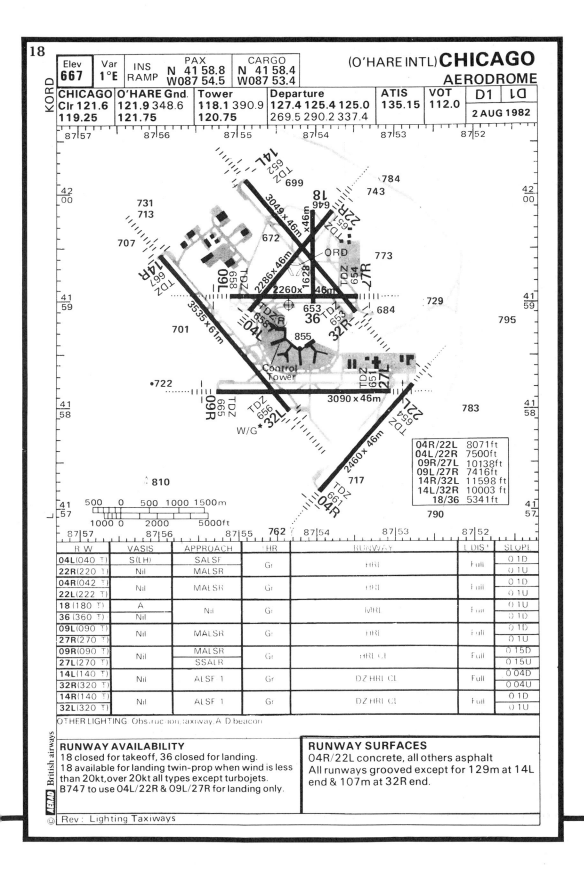

(O'HARE INTL) CHICAGO
AERODROME

KORD

Elev **667**	Var **1°E**	INS RAMP	PAX N 41 58.8 W087 54.5	CARGO N 41 58.4 W087 53.4			D1	D1
CHICAGO Clr **121.6** **119.25**	O'HARE Gnd. **121.9** 348.6 **121.75**	Tower **118.1** 390.9 **120.75**	Departure **127.4 125.4 125.0** 269.5 290.2 337.4		ATIS **135.15**	VOT **112.0**		**2 AUG 1982**

Runway lengths:

04R/22L	8071ft
04L/22R	7500ft
09R/27L	10138ft
09L/27R	7416ft
14L/32L	11598 ft
14L/32R	10003 ft
18/36	5341ft

R W	VASIS	APPROACH	HR	RUNWAY	L DIS	SLOPE
04L(040 T)	S(LH)	SALSF	Gr	HRl	Full	0 1D
22R(220 T)	Nil	MALSR				0 1U
04R(042 T)	Nil	MALSR	Gr	HRl	Full	0 1D
22L(222 T)						0 1U
18 (180 T)	A	Nil	Gr	MRl	Full	0 1U
36 (360 T)	Nil					0 1D
09L(090 T)	Nil	MALSR	Gr	HRl	Full	0 1D
27R(270 T)						0 1U
09R(090 T)	Nil	MALSR	Gr	HRl Cl	Full	0 15D
27L(270 T)		SSALR				0 15U
14L(140 T)	Nil	ALSF 1	Gr	DZ HRl Cl	Full	0 04D
32R(320 T)						0 04U
14R(140 T)	Nil	ALSF 1	Gr	DZ HRl Cl	Full	0 1D
32L(320 T)						0 1U

OTHER LIGHTING Obstruction, taxiway, A D beacon

RUNWAY AVAILABILITY
18 closed for takeoff, 36 closed for landing.
18 available for landing twin-prop when wind is less than 20kt, over 20kt all types except turbojets.
B747 to use 04L/22R & 09L/27R for landing only.

RUNWAY SURFACES
04R/22L concrete, all others asphalt
All runways grooved except for 129m at 14L end & 107m at 32R end.

British airways

© Rev: Lighting Taxiways

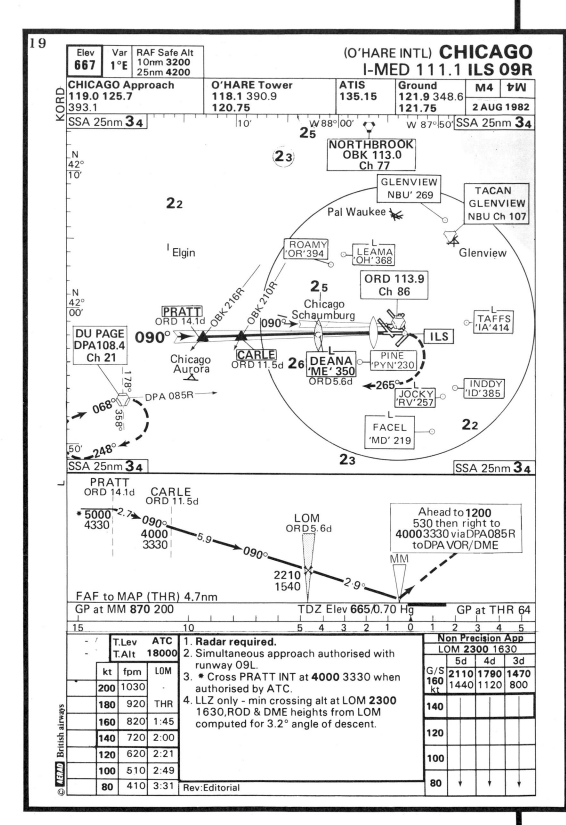

(O'HARE INTL) **CHICAGO**
I-MED 111.1 ILS 09R

Elev **667**	Var **1°E**	RAF Safe Alt 10nm **3200** 25nm **4200**

CHICAGO Approach 119.0 125.7 393.1	O'HARE Tower 118.1 390.9 120.75	ATIS 135.15	Ground 121.9 348.6 121.75	M4	M4
					2 AUG 1982

KORD

SSA 25nm **34**

NORTHBROOK
OBK 113.0
Ch 77

GLENVIEW
NBU' 269

TACAN
GLENVIEW
NBU Ch 107

Pal Waukee

Glenview

N 42° 10'

2 2

I Elgin

ROAMY 'OR' 394

L LEAMA 'OH' 368

ORD 113.9
Ch 86

L TAFFS 'IA' 414

N 42° 00'

2 5
Chicago
Schaumburg

OBK 216R

OBK 210R

090°

PRATT
ORD 14.1d

DU PAGE
DPA108.4
Ch 21

090°

Chicago
Aurora

CARLE
ORD 11.5d

ILS

2 6

L **DEANA**
'ME' 350
ORD 5.6d

PINE
'PYN' 230

←265°

L JOCKY 'RV' 257

INDDY 'ID' 385

178°
068°
358°
248°

DPA 085R →

L FACEL
'MD' 219

2 2

50'

SSA 25nm **34**

2 3

SSA 25nm **34**

PRATT
ORD 14.1d

CARLE
ORD 11.5d

*5000
4330 2.7

090°
4000
3330

5.9

090°

LOM
ORD 5.6d

Ahead to **1200**
530 then right to
4000 3330 via DPA 085R
to DPA VOR/DME

2210
1540

2·9°

MM

FAF to MAP (THR) 4.7nm

GP at MM **870** 200

TDZ Elev **665**/0.70 Hg

GP at THR 64

| 15 | 10 | 5 | 4 | 3 | 2 | 1 | 0 | 1 | 2 | 3 | 4 | 5 |

British airways

	T.Lev **18000**	ATC	**Non Precision App**

	T.Lev T.Alt	ATC 18000
kt	fpm	LOM
200	1030	-
180	920	THR
160	820	1:45
140	720	2:00
120	620	2:21
100	510	2:49
80	410	3:31

1. **Radar required.**
2. Simultaneous approach authorised with runway 09L.
3. * Cross PRATT INT at **4000** 3330 when authorised by ATC.
4. LLZ only - min crossing alt at LOM **2300** 1630, ROD & DME heights from LOM computed for 3.2° angle of descent.

Rev:Editorial

Non Precision App			
LOM **2300** 1630			
	5d	**4d**	**3d**
G/S 160 kt	2110 1440	1790 1120	1470 800
140			
120			
100			
80	↓	↓	↓

© AERAD

Engineer draws the thrust levers back to idle. Speedbird 298 is now, literally, a giant glider.

First Officer R/T 'Cleveland, Speedbird two ninety eight, out of three five oh for level two four oh.'
Cleveland R/T 'Thank you, two ninety eight.'

As the indicated airspeed builds up to 280kt the speed lock is engaged and the aircraft settles in the descent.

First Officer 'Altimeter check.'
All crew 'Out of three zero zero for two four zero.'

Further altimeter checks will be called at 10,000ft intervals.

Cleveland R/T 'Speedbird two ninety eight, call Chicago now one thirty two three.'

The selection is made.

First Officer R/T 'Chicago, Speedbird two ninety eight heavy, out of three hundred for level two four oh.'
Chicago R/T 'Speedbird two ninety eight, thank you. Down to ten thousand now, three zero three four. Cross Pappi level ten thousand.'

In North America the transition level everywhere is 180, and below this all heights are indicated in thousands of feet with the area pressure setting selected on the altimeter. Today's Chicago area pressure is 30.34in of mercury and is set by the pilot on both altimeters as Speedbird 298 is cleared below the transition level.

ATIS transmissions are now being received from Chicago and the Flight Engineer copies information 'golf', the 2200 GMT weather, which he passes foward to the Captain. The cloud is scattered at 5,000ft, visibility 9 statute miles, temperature 55°F, wind 040/10, altimeter pressure setting 30.34, and runways 09L, 09R, and 04R in use. On VHF2 now the Flight Engineer dials the Chicago company frequency of 131.1MHz and transmits the estimated landing time of 2231 GMT, and an on the gate estimate of 2240, 5min early on schedule. The company in turn passes back the gate number with a request to call ramp frequency 129.05MHz on arrival.

Fig 19:
Chicago O'Hare runway 09R approach.

These transmissions are unheard by the pilots who are listening out to ATC on VHF1, so the Flight Engineer informs the Captain that gate bravo 5 has been allocated.

At 65nm north of Pappi Speedbird 298 passes level 240 and continues descent to 10 to be level at Pappi. Some power is now applied by the Captain to slow the rate of descent to 1,000ft/min

Chicago R/T 'Speedbird two ninety eight, Chicago now, one thirty three two.'

The Co-pilot selects 133.2MHz but has to wait for a gap to break through the almost continuous flow of conversation.

First Officer R/T 'Chicago, Speedbird two ninety eight heavy, out of two four oh for ten thousand.'

Chicago R/T 'Speedbird two ninety eight heavy, cleared Pappi ten thousand to cross Pappi level.'
First Officer H/T 'Speedbird two ninety eight, cross Pappi level ten thousand.'

The Captain lifts the handset for some words with the passengers.

Captain PA 'Ladies and Gentlemen, the Captain. We're now well on our descent into Chicago. There's quite a lot of traffic around, but we don't expect any significant delays, so we should be on the ground in about twenty minutes and on the gate shortly afterwards. The weather is fine, fresh wind from the north east, and the temperature is 55° Fahrenheit, that's 13° centigrade.'

A second altimeter check is called by the Co-pilot at 20,000ft and all respond 'twenty thousand for ten'.

Chicago R/T 'Speedbird two ninety eight, maintain ten on reaching. After Pappi direct O'Hare VOR.'
First Officer R/T 'Speedbird two ninety eight, maintain ten thousand, after Pappi direct O'Hare VOR.'

The INS is tracking the aircraft towards Pappi, just over 30nm away, with the autopilot engaged, but the pilots are still required to monitor progress by mapping a mental picture of aircraft position from instruments, and the position of other flights from radio communications. Keeping one's mind ahead of the aircraft at all times is the secret of good operation. The pace is fast on jets and it's too easy to get left behind the aeroplane.

'Altitude green' is called by all as the autopilot captures 10,000ft, and over Pappi the INS is disengaged and 'november juliet' turned for the O'Hare VOR using the heading control knob. In the States the maximum speed for all traffic below 10,000ft is 250kt, and since the aircraft is aerodynamically smooth, losing speed takes time and speed reduction is begun at this point.

Chicago R/T 'Speedbird two ninety eight, traffic twelve o'clock, northeast bound, slow moving, height unknown.'
First Officer R/T 'Thank you, Speedbird two ninety eight, we're looking.'

The outline of the far shore of Lake Michigan can be seen in the distance but with the sun setting traffic lookout is difficult. The US has many light aircraft flying and a controller often has in view on his radar screen a number of unidentified blips. Any traffic in the vicinity is brought to the pilot's attention by a controller indicating the position of aircraft relative to the pilot using the hours of the clock, 12 o'clock being dead ahead. With such intensity of light traffic lower airspace in the States is jokingly referred to as 'Indian territory'.

Settled at 250kt power is applied and the speed maintained by the Flight Engineer.

Chicago R/T 'Speedbird two ninety eight, call approach now one nineteen zero.'
First Officer R/T 'Good day.'
First Officer R/T 'Chicago approach, Speedbird two ninety eight heavy, level ten thousand with information "golf".'

On approach frequency the pace hots up and the volume of radio chatter further increases. Approach does not reply and Speedbird 298 appears to be ignored as the controller vectors a number of flights ahead.

Chicago Approach R/T 'United two oh four, left one eight zero, down to six thousand. American five oh two heavy, right two seven zero, recleared eight thousand. Air Canada four oh six turn left one two zero, recleared three thousand. Cleared to intercept the nine right localiser. Call the tower now, one eighteen one. Speedbird two ninety eight heavy, right heading two five oh, vectors for nine right, speed two ten knots . . .'

How the controller manages to keep up such a

Fig 20:
Chicago O'Hare area radio Navigation chart.

flow of instructions is unbelievable. There just isn't time for pilots or controller to reply formally to all communications and aircraft are simply expected to comply, although movements are carefully monitored by radar. In fact, in the States emphasis on radar control is very strong. In Europe, for example, radar tends to be used as a monitor of the flight's progress rather than to direct aircraft, except on the approach phase of the flight where practices are similar to America. Aircraft are picked off by radar at specified points and vectored by headings on to the instrument landing system. S-bends, and even complete circles, are flown under radar instruction for sequencing of flights to maintain required separation. Headings, heights and speeds are all flown to ATC requirements. On departure and en route in Europe, however, aircraft normally adhere to allocated standard instrument departure routeings and follow flight plan routes while monitored by radar, except, on occasions, when radar headings are issued if a re-routeing becomes necessary or a level change is required on a busy airway. In the States it is quite different. Departure instructions normally just specify a climb to a certain height on runway heading and as soon as the aircraft is in the air radar control takes over and directs the flight by radar headings to the required airway. Sometimes complete flights over US airspace are conducted without following the flight plan route, the aircraft being continuously issued headings to steer by radar while the flight is passed from controller to controller along the way.

The Captain now calls for flap one degree as he eases back the thrust levers to reduce speed. The Co-pilot checks the speed, selects flap one degree, and checks that the flaps are set.

First Officer 'Flap one set.'
Captain 'Approach check please.'

The Flight Engineer proceeds with the approach check. Cabin signs are switched on, boost pumps are switched on, cross feed valves are checked set for landing, ignition is set to flight start, auto brakes are set to minimum, and altimeter settings are checked. The approach is not considered finished until 5° flap is set, but all other items are complete.

Chicago Approach R/T 'Speedbird two

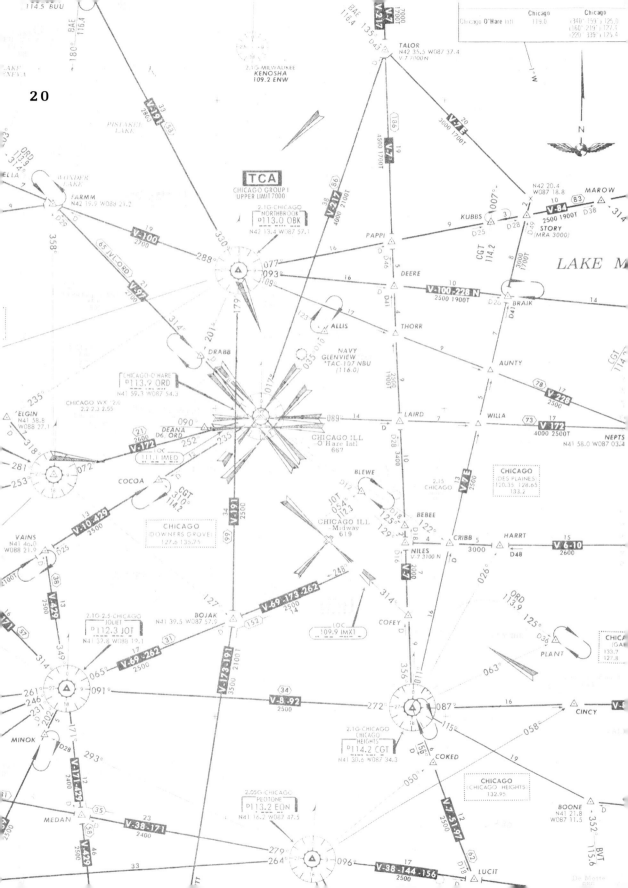

DESCENT AND LANDING DATA 747					British airways
AIRFIELD: CHICAGO O'HARE	RUNWAY: 09R	QNH 3034			mbs / ins
EST. LANDING WEIGHT 220·2 KGS		SAFETY HEIGHT		3400	FT.

V REF 130 KTS	MIN SPEED +10 140	SECTOR SAFETY ALT	3400	QNH
MIN. SPEED 130 KTS	V REF +40 170	TRANSITION LEVEL	180	FL
FOR	V REF +80 210	START FINAL APPROACH ALTITUDE	5000	QNH
A/C CONFIG 30 °FLAP		O.M. HEIGHT	2210	QNH

MAX. GO AROUND	EPR 1·41	APPROACH	D.H./QNH	RVR/VIS	D.H./R.A.
FUEL AT DESTINATION	20,200 KGS	ILSC2	/////		
		ILSC			
DIVERSION FUEL TO DETROIT	11,900 KGS	ILSH	970'	4000'	/////

	HRS MINS	
HOLDING FUEL	0 : 50 8,300 KGS	OVERSHOOT HT. 4000' QNH
REG. LANDING WEIGHT MAX. KGS		
21		AIRFIELD ELEVATION 667 FT.

ninety eight heavy, right heading two seven zero, down to six thousand, speed back to one eighty knots.'

The Captain turns the heading control knob to 270° and eases the aircraft into a gentle descent using the autopilot vertical control wheel. 6,000ft is set in altitude select. The final altimeter check is called leaving 10,000ft for six.

Captain 'Flap five, please.'

Flap 5° is selected, and when checked and set the Flight Engineer announces the approach check complete. The speed is reduced to 180kt.

The 09R instrument landing system (ILS) frequency of 111.1MHz is now selected on both sides and identified from the I-MED morse coding. The ILS transmits a pattern of horizontal and vertical lobes of energy that give runway centre line (known as localiser) and approach path guidance right down to touchdown. On the artificial horizon, flight director horizontal and vertical yellow bars give, when selected, aircraft position relative to the ILS, and when crossed in the middle indicate the aircraft to be properly established on the radio beams. The precise runway centre line direction of 090° magnetic is also set in the course indicator

Fig 21:
Descent and Landing Data.

Above right:
In case of early descent the Captain now calls for the 'before descent check'.

windows. Runways are, in fact, named by rounding the precise direction to the nearest 10 degrees and omitting the last zero. Runway 09R happens to be exactly 090°, but the right northeasterly runway, for example, is 042° magnetic direction, which becomes 040°, which becomes 04. Parallel runways are named left or right, hence 04R. The locator outer marker beacon, Deana, frequency 350KHz, is selected on both automatic direction finders and identified. The height to cross the outer marker is also noted as 2,210ft, and time to touchdown from the beacon just over 2min at an approach of approximately 135kt.

'One thousand to go' is called as 7,000ft is passed on the descent to six. Below, the ground can be seen clearly now in the still daylight conditions, and horizontal visibility is excellent.

Chicago Approach 'Speedbird two ninety eight heavy, turn left heading one eight oh.'

As the big jet turns the Captain applies more power to slow the rate of descent. The volume of radio communications is still high as a number of aircraft are being vectored simultaneously for landing. Some are landing on the parallel runway 09L and even the odd one on 04R. Such approaches at busy airports result in high workload for the controllers, but are also hectic for flight crews, especially those cleared worldwide who may only visit such places on the rare occasion. Short sectors in the States can be just as intense in heavy traffic and can also be rushed for crews who may not have flown the route for some time. Boston-Philadelphia is one, where the flight from London transits Boston, and the crew have to cope with a short busy sector after a tiring Atlantic crossing — like driving, after a long journey, through a busy city one hasn't visited too often.

Chicago Approach R/T 'Speedbird two ninety eight heavy, turn left heading one two oh. Recleared three thousand. Cleared nine right approach. Speed minimum one sixty to the marker. Call the tower one eighteen one at the marker.'

3,000ft is set in the altitude select window. The Captain calls 'disconnecting the autopilot' and presses the button to assume manual control. As 'november juliet' is turned to head

120° a selection is made on the flight director switching to display ILS presentation on instruments.

Captain 'Flap ten please.'

The Co-pilot checks the speed and selects flap 10° while once again being monitored by the Flight Engineer.

As the First Officer calls 'beam bar active' the Captain banks the aircraft left to fly the localiser and 'nav green' is called as runway centre line tracking is established. Shortly Speedbird 298 levels at 3,000ft and altitude green lights illuminate indicating flight director capture. The horizontal glide path bar is now seen to move from the stops.

First Officer 'Glide path active.'
Captain 'Flap twenty, please,'

As the Co-pilot selects flap 20° the glide path green lights illuminate indicating capture and the altitude green lights extinguish. The Captain lowers the nose to fly the ILS and eases off some power to maintain 170kt.

First Officer 'Drift nine degrees right.'

The wind is blowing from the north east and the Captain is having to crab the aircraft

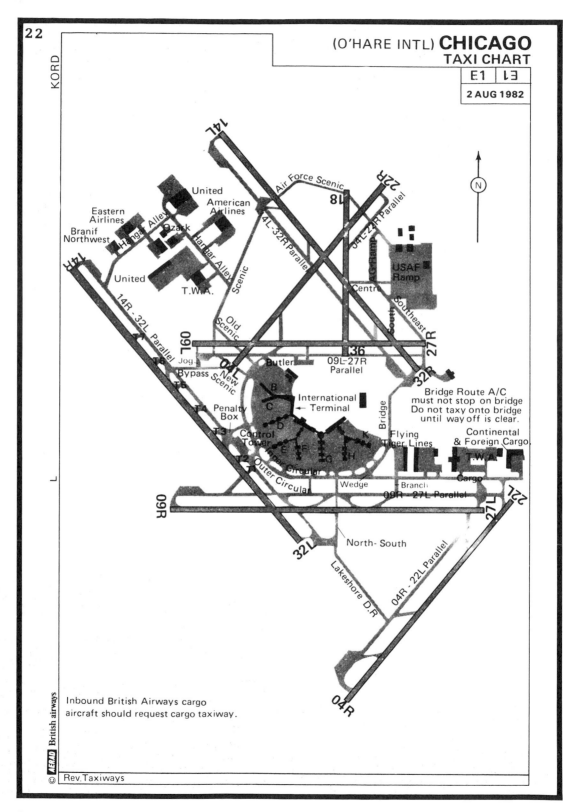

(O'HARE INTL) **CHICAGO**
TAXI CHART

E1 | ⅃Ε

2 AUG 1982

N

14L

Air Force Scenic

22R

18

United
American
Airlines

Eastern
Airlines

Branif
Northwest

Hangar Alley

Ozark

Hangar Alley

United

T.W.A.

4L-32R Parallel

Scenic

Old
Scenic

04L-22R Parallel

AG Ramp

USAF
Ramp

Centre

South

Southeast

27R

14R

14R - 32L Parallel

760

09L

Jog

Bypass

New Scenic

36

09L-27R
Parallel

32R

T6

T5

T4

Penalty
Box

Butler

International
Terminal

B

C

D

Bridge

Bridge Route A/C
must not stop on bridge
Do not taxy onto bridge
until way off is clear.

T3

Control
Tower

E

F

G

H

K

Flying
Tiger Lines

Continental
& Foreign Cargo

T.W.A.

T2

Inner Circular

Outer Circular

Wedge

Branch

Cargo

T1

09R

09R - 27L Parallel

27L

22L

32L

North- South

Lakeshore D.R

04R - 22L Parallel

04R

British airways

Inbound British Airways cargo
aircraft should request cargo taxiway.

© Rev. Taxiways

L

along the localiser to maintain runway centre line.

Passing 2,500ft the Captain calls for the 'landing check.' The gear is selected down and checked locked, the spoilers/speed brakes are armed to automatically deploy at touchdown to 'spoil' the lift, and a last check of the hydraulics by the Flight Engineer is made to confirm systems satisfactory. The landing check is called complete. Over the outer marker the automatic direction finder needles swing round, the stopwatch is started, and the glide path height of 2,240ft is checked. The First Officer selects 118.1MHz.

First Officer R/T 'Tower, Speedbird two ninety eight heavy, outer marker inbound.'
Chicago Tower 'Speedbird two ninety eight heavy, continue approach.'

Speedbird 298 is now four miles from the threshold and ahead an aircraft can be seen just touching down on 09R. To the left an aircraft on approach to 09L is seen about two miles from touchdown, while another at the

Fig 22:
Chicago O'Hare Taxi chart.

Below:
The safety height is also confirmed as 3,400ft. The land around O'Hare is in fact, quite flat, but the tall skyscrapers of the city lying to the southeast of the airport result in the safety height being high.

end of its landing run on 04R is seen just leaving the runway. One aircraft is also noticed just lifting off from 09L. Five aircraft, including 'november juliet' in the process of landing and taking off at the same time!

The pressure altimeter now indicates Speedbird 298 passing 1,900ft with the radio altimeter showing 1,230ft to touchdown (ie airport elevation 670ft).

First Officer 'Drift seven degrees right.'

The Captain has his left hand on the control column continuously making slight adjustments to fly the ILS. His right hand is on the thrust levers adjusting power as required while feet are resting lightly on the rudder pedals in preparation for landing. At each flight stage trimming is required and is adjusted by a thumb switch on the control column. During the approach the Co-pilot makes the appropriate calls throughout while the whole procedure is monitored by the Flight Engineer.

Captain 'Full flap, please.'

The First Officer selects full flap 30° and the nose drops as flaps run out. The Captain now lets the speed drop back to the final approach speed of about 135kt, and a clicking is heard from the trim wheel as aircraft trim is adjusted. The First Officer is now watching the radio altimeter.

First Officer   'One thousand feet check. Gear is down, full flap set, no instrument failure flags, missed approach height of four thousand feet set.'

The calls are confirmed by the other two crew members. Speedbird 298 is now three miles from touchdown. With the nose pitched down the view over the instrument panel is improved and the vast expanse of O'Hare can be seen stretching in front. In the distance the skyscrapers of Chicago pierce the late afternoon winter sky. At two miles from touchdown 'november juliet' is cleared to land. The landing aircraft ahead clears the runway, and landing is now at the discretion of the Captain.

First Officer   'One hundred to decision.'

The pressure altimeter shows 1,070ft with the radio altimeter indicating 400ft. At 970ft the Co-pilot calls decision height.

Captain   'Continuing.'
First Officer   'One hundred feet.'

Top:
Speedbird 298 is now, literally, a giant glider.

Above:
Some power is now applied by the Captain to slow the rate of descent to 1,000ft per minute.

Fig 23:
Chicago O'Hare ramp chart.

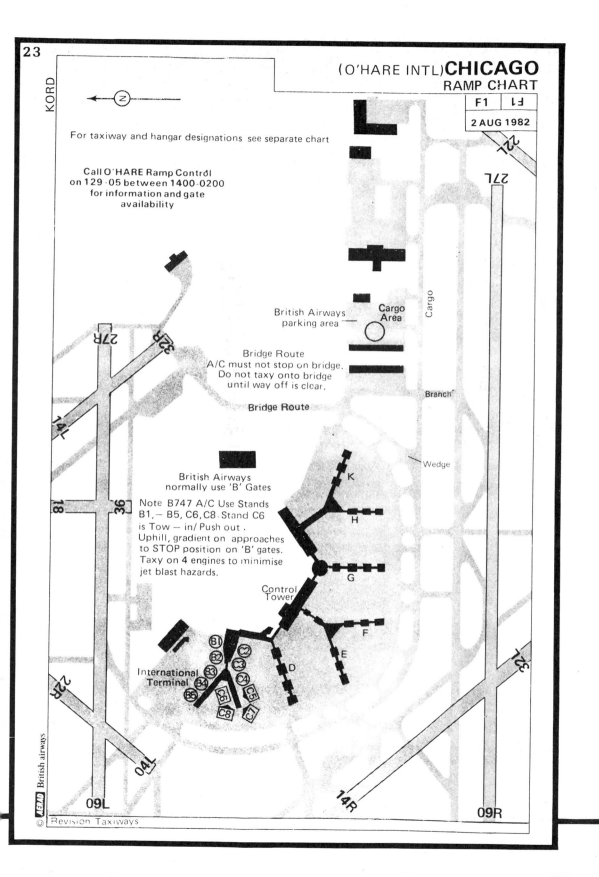

KORD

For taxiway and hangar designations see separate chart

Call O'HARE Ramp Control
on 129·05 between 1400-0200
for information and gate
availability

F1   F1

2 AUG 1982

British Airways
parking area

Cargo
Area

Cargo

Bridge Route
A/C must not stop on bridge.
Do not taxy onto bridge
until way off is clear.

Bridge Route

Branch

Wedge

British Airways
normally use 'B' Gates

Note B747 A/C Use Stands
B1, — B5, C6, C8. Stand C6
is Tow — in/ Push out .
Uphill, gradient on approaches
to STOP position on 'B' gates.
Taxy on 4 engines to minimise
jet blast hazards.

K

H

G

Control
Tower

F

E

D

International
Terminal

B1
B2
B3
B4
B5
C2
C3
C4
C6
C8
C5
C7

27R

32R

14L

18

36

27L

27L

32L

22R

04L

09L

14R

09R

Above:
The INS is tracking the aircraft towards Pappi, just over 30nm away.

Left:
'Tower, Speedbird Two Ninety Eight heavy, outer marker inbound.'

The call is made from the radio altimeter as the threshold markings flash beneath the nose.

First Officer   Fifty feet.' . . . 'Thirty feet.'

The Captain eases back on the control column to 'flare' the aircraft by arresting the rate of descent while at the same time closing the thrust levers with the right hand. A touch of right rudder is applied to straighten the nose. The aircraft hangs momentarily above the ground before a sudden rumble is heard as the main wheels touch, and the aircraft sits heavily on the runway with deployment of the spoilers. The main wheels spin up and the auto brakes begin to bite. The Captain's left hand plays the control column, gently lowering the nose wheel, while the right hand moves forward to the reverse thrust levers. The levers are pulled back to a stop while doors within the engine casing position to deflect fan air forward about 45° through cascade vanes. With the blocker doors in place mechanical locks retract and the Captain pulls on full reverse. The engines roar in response. Another rumble is heard as the nose wheel touches and Speedbird 298 is down. The Captain steers the aircraft along the runway centre line by delicate movement of the rudder pedals while the First Officer calls the speeds as the jet slows.

First Officer 'Eighty knots, seventy, sixty, fifty . . .'

Reverse thrust is cancelled, and as the aircraft speed drops below 30kt the Captain transfers his left hand to the tiller for nose wheel steering while body gear steering is selected in preparation for taxi. Braking is now manual via the toe brakes.

Chicago Tower R/T 'Speedbird two ninety eight, exit left at the end. Call ground point nine when clear.'
First Officer 'Good day.'

121.9MHz is selected.

As Speedbird 298 leaves the runway the Captain calls for the 'after landing' check. Body gear steering is checked armed, auto brakes checked off, spoilers are selected in, flaps are selected to zero, the transponder is set to standby, probe heat is switched off, etc . . . a general tidying of aircraft systems is carried out.

First Officer R/T 'Ground, Speedbird two ninety eight heavy is clear nine right.'

Chicago Ground R/T 'Speedbird two ninety eight heavy, turn left down the nine right parallel taxiway. Transfer to the outer circular taxiway at Branch.'

Taxying along the 09R parallel, the Captain has a last few words with the passengers welcoming them to Chicago.

Captain PA 'Ladies and Gentlemen, Captain Murray. Welcome to Chicago. We have quite a long taxi ahead of us so it will be a few more minutes before we arrive at the gate. I hope you've enjoyed your trip with us. I'll say goodbye now and wish you all a pleasant stay.'

At Branch, 'november juliet' transfers to the outer circular and proceeds to the international gate behind a line of jets taxying from the domestic terminals for departure on 04L. Speedbird 298 transfers to the inner circular taxiway at T3, then turns sharp right by the international terminal to enter the 'bravo' ramp area. Abeam gate bravo 5 the Captain turns right again and taxies gently forward, under the guidance of a marshaller, to park nose in. At the exact spot the marshaller crosses the batons above his head and the aircraft is brought to a halt. The brakes are set to park, the engines shut down, and the 'leaving aircraft check' commenced. 129.05MHz is called to confirm gate arrival at 2242 GMT, three minutes early on schedule. Aircraft systems are shut down in turn, but before the INS is switched off an accuracy check is made and details noted. Numbers 1, 2 and 3 sets are shown to be out 7nm, 4nm and 1nm respectively — not bad after 3,559nm. With all systems shut down, radio equipment switched off, instrument panels reset, and flight deck tidied, the crew are free to leave. The aircraft has just under four hours before returning to London, but the crew, at least, have the chance of a rest.

In the arrivals hall immigration and customs formalities are completed, and the crew bus then boarded for the journey to a hotel. On arrival allowances for meals are paid in local currency at reception. It is still daylight in Chicago, but GMT is now midnight. The six-hour time change is a tiring experience, but crews, generally, try to keep to local time and arrangements are made to meet in the lobby at 6.30pm (12.30am London time!) to go out for a few drinks. It is decided to head for She-nannigan's on Division Street, one of a number of lively bars in the area.

Chicago is a fine city with a fabulous museum, beautiful art gallery and exciting night life. The city hosts the world's biggest commodity market, boasts the world's tallest skyscraper (Sear's Tower) and encloses the famous elevated downtown Loop, an overhead railway system which embraces the commercial heart of the city. Unfortunately crews are usually too tired to enjoy the attractions, not to mention the lack of time for sightseeing on short stopovers. A few beers in the evening are usually followed by falling exhausted into bed, with the inevitable early waking in the morning because of the time change. The day then normally begins with a hearty American breakfast. After shopping in the morning it's back to bed once more in the afternoon in an attempt to get some sleep for the night flight ahead. Pick up from the hotel is at 6.45pm for an 08.30 departure from O'Hare. The whole process is then repeated flying the aircraft back to London, arriving in Heathrow at 10 the next morning. Very tired!

Right:
Chicago Tower — 'Speedbird Two Ninety Eight heavy, continue approach.' The Tower Controller monitors approaches to the nine right and left runways on the radar scope.

Below:
Controllers monitor positions around the Tower. Long leads to head-sets allow the Controllers to move about freely.

Bottom:
The skyline of Chicago seen from the Control Tower.

Left:
Passing 2,000ft. Gear locked down, flap twenty set.

Inset:
1,500 . . . the skyline of Chicago seen from the right window. Full flap selected.

Bottom:
'Final approach.'

Below:
'One thousand feet check.'

Above:
'Short Finals' . . . 'november juliet' is cleared to land.

Left:
'One hundred to decision.'

Below:
The Co-pilot calls decision height.

Left:
Over the approach lights.

Below:
'One hundred feet.'

Bottom:
Over the threshold. 'Fifty feet.' Shot from behind between the approach lighting.

Below:
'Thirty feet.'

Left:
The Captain eases back on the control column to 'flare' the aircraft.

Below centre:
Touch down. Smoke from the tyres can be seen below the tail.

Bottom:
. . . a sudden rumble is heard as the main wheels touch . . .

Above:
'November juliet' proceeds to the International Gate behind a line of jets ...

Below:
... taxying from the domestic terminal for departure on 04L.

Bottom:
Speedbird 298 transfers to the inner circular taxiway at T3 ...

Below:
The Captain turns right again ...

Left:
. . . and proceeds on the inner circular . . .

Below:
. . . then turns sharp right by the international terminal to enter the 'bravo' ramp area.

Above left:
. . . and taxies gently forward . . .

Left:
. . . to park nose in.

Above:
129.05MHz is called to confirm gate arrival at 22.42. Speedbird 298 seen at the gate from the Tower.

Right:
Wheels are confirmed chocked . . . (Note the turn-off lights and the gear doors)

Top:
. . . steps are placed in position . . .

Above:
. . . and the passengers cleared to disembark.

Right:
Passengers proceeding to the terminal building.

Below:
Disembarkation complete.

Above:
Chicago and Lake Michigan looking north from the top of Sear's Tower. The masts of the Hancock Building can be seen cutting the Horizon.

Left:
The famous elevated downtown Loop.

...CHICAGO